STYLE SOURCE IRELAND – INTERIORS

First published in 2006 by
CURRACH PRESS
55A Spruce Avenue, Stillorgan Industrial Park, Blackrock, Co. Dublin

www.currach.ie

1 3 5 4 2

Cover by Sin é Design
Origination by Richard Parfrey
Printed by Estudios Gráficos ZURE, Bizkaia, Spain
ISBN: 1-85607-944-9

Front cover photographs, from top: chair by Casa Milano at **Minima**; lamp and chest by Ensemble at **Milo Fitzgerald**; bed and lamp from **Living**; lamp by Paul Costelloe at **Dunnes Home**; shelving by Casa Milano at **Minima**.

Back cover photographs (clockwise from top left): vases from **Habitat**; kitchen by **Snaidero**; light from **Classic Furniture**; sofa from **Living**; chest from **Classic Furniture**; bath by **Driftwood**; chaise by Natuzzi at **Arnotts**; bed from **Brown Thomas.**

Opening photograph in Bedroom section: Alan Betson
Opening photograph in Special Things section: Alan Betson; styling Catherine Condell; make-up: Christine Lucignano.

STYLE SOURCE IRELAND – INTERIORS

WHERE TO BUY THE BEST FURNISHINGS FOR YOUR HOME

EOIN LYONS

CURRACH PRESS

FOREWORD

Alexandra McGuinness

Dorothy Parker said, 'A little bad taste is like a dash of paprika.'

I tend to agree with her.

There is a girl inside me that loves everything gaudy and tacky. In an ideal world, I'd give her a small allowance and let her buy bits and pieces of tat from markets, auctions and (eeek!) Ebay.

Last year, though, when I looked around my flat in London it seemed like that girl inside me might have taken over. I had collected an almighty amount of junk. All the dealers at Portobello market knew me by name, my Ebay profile had garnered a green star and two hundred comments of positive feedback from sellers, and my flatmate shuddered every time the postman knocked on the door.

Zebra-skin rugs, reindeer-skin rugs, a mirror ball, miniature statues of all five of the Marx brothers, an illuminated 1960s corner bar complete with umbrella and bar stools, sequinned curtains, stacks of garish patchwork quilts, a gold-lamé-covered spittoon, fairy lights everywhere, at least twenty Schiaparelli pink hat boxes, a red-and-gold lacquered corner desk without a corner to sit in, Mexican dollhouses, an armchair that Laura Ashley had puked on and my personal favourite: a stuffed alligator holding a parasol under one arm and a suitcase under the other. But still I stayed up late into the night bidding for neon signs on Ebay. I held a secret envy of a friend who had a bigger flat and two of the holy grails of junk – a working juke-box and a giant index finger – bought from a manicure shop that was going out of business.

I was drowning in paprika.

You may remember from a previous bestseller that God sent a great flood to rid the world of the bad and brutal. Well, in my story Thames water did the same thing. I was in Toronto trying to convince some pharmacists to invest money in my movie about midget gymnasts in love when my flatmate, Nana, called me. She informed me that my beloved basement flat was submerged under three foot of dubious-smelling water. I may have omitted to tell you that I neglected to install anything useful like shelves or storm drains.

I returned home to a very sad scene, a soggy flat with dehumidifiers at full blast and all my treasured junk destroyed. (I'm not even going to mention my clothes and shoes – time has not healed the wounds.) All the taxidermy had turned into scaly mush, Harpo Marx had lost his head, the vast amounts of Lloyd loom wicker furniture had disintegrated, my heather-purple velvet sofa had turned to an olive-green shade and the neon lights could not be touched for fear of death by electrocution.

Nana and I sat in our temporary dwellings and mourned our material losses. But every cloud has a silver lining… Both of us are writers and, as such, we were sitting down to a busy afternoon of *Countdown* and *Grazia* magazine when an envelope floated down from the letterbox. Inside were two rather sizeable cheques. In a move of uncharacteristic brilliance I had taken out contents insurance. My cheque was a lot larger than Nana's.

My junk turned out to be a goldmine.

Now I am reinstated in my beloved basement flat and it is considerably less cluttered. There are shelves on the slipper-satin walls and the beautiful limestone floor is now visible. I could have taken my big fat cheque and indulged the tacky girl inside but instead I showed restraint and invested in floor-to-ceiling shoe racks. I took the rest of the money and flew off to Kenya for six weeks of rest and recuperation where I developed a minor fetish for camel-skin table lamps, but that's another story.

I finish where I started with Dorothy Parker, who once noted, 'There are certain bachelors who inspire in women an unstoppable urge to start presenting swathes of chintz and books of wallpaper patterns.'

Eoin Lyons is indeed one of these bachelors (although chintz and wallpaper may not be quite his thing) and this book is an invaluable tool for those seeking to feather their nests. As Eoin will show you it doesn't need to cost the Earth; let him point you in the direction of comfortable, tasteful, imaginative beds, chairs and tables, luxurious curtains and one-of-a-kind lamps. All put together with a certain indefinable, special something that Eoin sums up like this: 'Live with what you love – that's what counts.' And if that happens to be a dash of paprika, so be it.

Alexandra McGuinness is an actress, writer and director.

INTRODUCTION

The idea of putting this book together came to me about a year ago when a friend who wanted to buy furniture couldn't think where to go in Ireland, beyond the obvious. So within these pages this friend and, I hope, you the reader will find details of both well and lesser-known retailers. *Style Source Ireland: Interiors* wasn't designed to be the last word on interiors shopping; nor can it claim to be comprehensive. Instead it's a personal guide to a number of places I consider worthwhile.

This book is about ideas, so try to use it creatively: you might find a bed in a shop listed in the Dining Room section, or vice versa. And use your imagination: a limited amount of space meant that I couldn't cover every furniture permutation, but I think you'll find anything you're looking for in some shop or other included here. Prices are quoted as a guide for when you visit (i.e. whether you'll need to sell the children, the car and the dog to buy a sofa). Similarly, the photographs simply show the kind of style in the featured shop, not necessarily current stock.

For *Style Source Ireland: Interiors* I've focused on furniture inside the home. Outdoor furniture is another story…

I hope you enjoy this book.

Eoin Lyons, October 2006

NOTE: Where a shop is mentioned more than once in a section, the address and other contact details are given only the first time. Full contact details for all suppliers are listed at the end of the book.

ACKNOWLEDGEMENTS

This book gives me an opportunity to thank a number of people who have helped me at various times and in different ways, many both professionally and personally:

Ann Bracken; Antonia Campbell Hughes; Ashleigh Downey; Barry Lyons; Conor Goodman; Deirdre Connolly; Evy Richard; Frances O'Rourke; Frances Power; Fr. Kevin Lyons; Gerard McDonnell; Helen Seymour; Ian Galvin; Jackie Hughes; Joanne Hynes; John Beattie; John Lyons; John Mahony; Jo O'Donoghue; Katherine Michael; Mary Andrews; Moira Downey; Michael Brennan; Orna Mulcahy; Paul J. Moley; Patsey Murphy; Phyl Clarke; Richard Parfrey; Robert O'Byrne; Sarah McDonnell; Sinéad McKenna; Sirin Lewendon; Sonia Reynolds; Teresa Daly; Tracy Tucker. And, of course, the Lyons brothers: Tom, Lorcan and Vincent.

This book would not have been possible without the wonderful generosity of Peter Thursfield at *The Irish Times*; Amanda Cochrane at *Image Interiors* and Rosemary Whelan at Ireland's *Antiques & Period Properties*, all of whom allowed me to use photographs from their archives. Thank you.

THE AUTHOR

Eoin Lyons was born in Dublin in 1976. An awareness of design was fostered in him at an early age by his architect father and interior-designer mother. He studied graphic design at the College of Marketing and Design in Mountjoy Square and began writing for *The Irish Times* in 2001, covering fashion initially. Since 2003 he has written about interiors and various other style-related topics for the same paper. He is a contributor to *Image Interiors* and has also written for UK publications including *House & Garden* and *LivingEtc*. Eoin also acts as a consultant to interior retailers and as a stylist on interiors shoots. He can be reached at elyons@irish-times.ie.

FOR MY PARENTS LORCAN AND FRANCES LYONS

Contents

Entrance Hall   **12**
Console Tables   14
Stair Coverings   17
Mirrors   18
Flowers   18
Storage   19

Living Room   **20**
Sofas   23
Mirrors   35
Coffee Tables   36
Screens   39
Side tables   40
Nests of tables   41

Dining Room   **42**
Tables   45
Chairs   50
Sideboards   54

Kitchen   **56**
Sources for worktops   66
Shelving   67
Stools   67
Breakfast Tables   68
Appliances   68

Bedroom   **70**
Beds   73
Fabric Headboards   80
Bedside Lockers and Dressing Tables   80
Footstools   81
Mattresses   81

Bedlinen   **82**
Wardrobes   84

Bathroom   **86**

Kids' Room   **100**

Home Office   **106**
Desks, Chairs and Desk Lights   109

THE MAN WHO BOUGHT HIS OWN FURNITURE (MICHAEL PARSONS)   111

SPECIAL THINGS   113
STYLE SOURCE: DON'T BE A SNOB   116
STYLE SOURCE: THE FRENCH LOOK   117
STYLE SOURCE: ASIAN   121
STYLE SOURCE: TRADITIONAL   123
STYLE SOURCE: ART DECO   128
STYLE SOURCE: 20TH-CENTURY FURNITURE   130
STYLE SOURCE: ECLECTIC CHIC   133
STYLE SOURCE: MODERN   134

AROUND THE HOUSE   138
ANTIQUES AND AUCTIONS   140
  ANTIQUES   140
  AUCTIONS   143
FLOORING   146
  CARPETS   146
  WOOD FLOORS   148
  STONE AND TILE   150
CURTAINS   150
  READY-MADE CURTAINS   151
  CURTAIN-MAKERS   152
FABRICS, PAINTS AND WALLPAPER   155
  SPECIALIST WALLPAPER   157
  WALL PAINT   158
LIGHTING   161
  LIGHT FITTINGS   162
HANGING PICTURES   169
FIREPLACES   173
STORAGE   173
  BOOKSHELVES   173
  BOXES AND BASKETS   176
  CHESTS OF DRAWERS   177
  CABINETS   178
SHOPPING IN BELFAST   179
GIFTS   181
CHRISTMAS   185

INTERIORITY COMPLEX (ORNA MULCAHY)   188
SUPPLIERS' CONTACT DETAILS   190

Entrance Hall

Every hall needs a good mirror, big enough for two. Models Rudi Kennedy and Nikki Bonass do last-minute checks in a 1940s mirror chosen by interior designer Joseph Ensko for a mews house on Raglan Lane in Dublin. Art deco dealer Niall Mullen will source something similar from his shop on Francis Street.

Top left: the entrance to the house of Brown Thomas board member Cecily MacMenamin has the essentail ingredients for a hall – a console table, a lamp and a chair.

Top rights: interior designer **Philippa Buckley's** hall. An antique console holds a pair of Murano glass lamps beneath a mirror by Knowles & Christou.

Bottom right: fashion and home-textile designer Helen McAlinden uses her two-drawer console to display some choice objects.

Bottom left: a typical console by Irish firm Sherry Furniture, from a line of traditional furniture available at **Arnotts**.

CONSOLE TABLES

'You only get one chance to make a first impression: an entrance hall sets the tone for your home. It can be daunting to think about an overall effect at once, so begin with a console table – choose one with authentic character. Halls tend not to have windows with a vista, so an enormous painting will provide views where none exist. Don't be shy about scale: one or two pictures can get lost on a wall, but a big painting takes you beyond the room. Add other things – a chair or lamps – as you can afford to over time.'

**Sirin Lewendon, interior designer
e-mail: sirin@sirinlewendon.com**

The hall needs…something. Maybe a spot is too dark, a corner too cluttered, a wall too bare. The answer is a console table, which can bring both a little extra style and a lot of practicality. Without the hefty imprint of a table, a console offers another surface just where it's needed. It supports a lamp, keys, post and more. The best consoles have spare elegant lines with an indispensable presence.

In the entrance hall of Cecily MacMenamin's Sandymount home a large glossy red lamp sits on a metal console. A chair is useful in a hall – her gilt chair was used at fashion shows from the 1950s to the 1980s at Brown Thomas. See the Dining Room section for lots of chair ideas.

Trawl Francis Street's antique shops for consoles you can mix with contemporary furniture. In her entrance hall interior designer Philippa Buckley uses an antique console from **Michael Connell Antiques** (54 Francis Street, Dublin 8. Tel: 01-4733898) with a bevelled mirror by Knowles & Christou. The mirror costs from €1950 and can be ordered through **www.studio44.ie**.

The Dublin Furniture Company (55 Capel Street, Dublin 1. Tel: 01-8728374) is a modest shop but usually has a few slender, very simple Indian hardwood console tables for about €300–€400. The stained finish lets the wood's imperfections come through, giving them a warm, handcrafted feel.

Another shop to try is **Robert Scott Designs** (59 Capel Street, Dublin 1. Tel: (01-8740654) for clean-lined oak-veneer consoles with drawers, that cost no more than about €400. Go to **Renaissance** (114 Capel Street, Dublin 1. Tel: 01-8873809) for neat marble-topped consoles (1920s, apparently) with ornate brass legs for about €300. Content by Conran is a range stocked at **Arnotts** (Henry Street, Dublin 1) that usually has natural wood consoles from €500. They're Zen, but groovy Zen.

The simple geometry of the Span table by furniture designer **Michael Bell** (Vicarstown, County Laois. Tel: 057-8625633 www.michaelbelldesign. com) is a winner. See his website for a picture. Inspired by bridges, the Span table can be customised to dimensions that suit your space and made in walnut, oak or maple.

Instore (Limerick, Tel: 061-416088; Waterford, Tel: 051-844882; Galway, Tel: 091-530085 and Sligo, Tel: 071-9149174) generally has traditional console tables at reasonable prices. For example, €189 will get you a dark-green-stained timber table with drawers and a natural oak top.

Look too at the shops in the Special section: most do consoles.

STAIR COVERINGS

If you're not a fan of carpet and don't want a noisy bare stairs, see the range of coloured sisal stair runners at **Limited Edition** (96 Francis Street, Dublin 8. Tel: 01-4531123). A nice one is the Chatham runner in Turkey red by Roger Oates. It's available in different widths and hard-wearing; it is also reversible so it gets a second life. Ulster Carpets at **Arnotts** do stair runners priced at €50 per square yard, which when felted, fitted and laid, work out at €95 per square yard.

Once used to hold carpets in place, stair rods are now purely decorative. **Martsworth Carpets** (Ashford, County Wicklow. Tel: 0404-40113) sell brass or wrought-iron rods from €55. There are also wooden rods, which tone well with natural weave and sisal runners. Chrome stair rods are €95 each...pricey for a whole stairs but they look great.

Top left: a hall decorated by **Merrion Square Interiors** – note the traditional curtaining of the doorway. Try **Décor** to find a similarly rustic table.

Top right: ceramic umbrella stands like the one pictured here can be found at **Esther Sexton Antiques** or **Michael Connell Antiques**.

Bottom right: a typically glam mirror and console table from **Minnie Peters**.

Bottom left: a custom-made console by Irish designers **Fassbinder & English**.

MIRRORS

Apart from a console, the essential item for a hall is a mirror. **Minnie Peters** (55 Upper George's Street, Dún Laoghaire, County Dublin. Tel: 01-2805965) is good for dramatic mirrors in large sizes, often framed in unusual leathers. The gilt-framed mottled mirror pictured on the previous page is typical of what's available. Something like this will cost €1700. See the Living Room section for a full list of mirror ideas.

FLOWERS

Administer the flower fix. Aim to have at least one good display near your front door. You've had a bad day: you come home, see flowers in your special vase and you just may feel better. Few people really need a cupboard full of vases, though. One that is magnificent will do, such as an Alvar Aalto smoked-glass vase for €175 at **Nordic Living** (Blackrock, County Dublin. Tel: 01-2886680, www.nordicliving.ie). Have fresh flowers on hand at all times. Don't wait to be sent them. My favourite florist is **Costello**

Top right: an Alvar Aalto vase from **Nordic Living**.

Centre right: 1930s consoles can be found at **theantiquewarehouse.ie**.

Bottom right: this console by Irish furniture designer **Charles O'Toole**, with tapered stainless steel legs, costs €1936.

Below: a metal coat stand from **Habitat**.

Opposite page: all dressed up – fashion designer Peter O'Brien's lady with console table.

Flowers (Northumberland Avenue, Dún Laoghaire, County Dublin. Tel: 01-2841864) – they do super-natural bouquets or high-drama sculptures, depending on your taste.

STORAGE

It's best to have a press to hold coats but if you do need a coat stand, go to **Habitat** (6-10 Suffolk Street, Dublin 2. Tel: 01-6771433; Fairgreen Road, Galway. Tel: 091-569980; and 41 Arthur Street, Belfast BT1 4GB. Tel: 028-90249522): they have a variety of cool metal versions from about €60. Or buy a couple of giant coat hanger 'paper clips' designed by **Leo Scarff** (see www.jist.ie). For shoes, **Inreda** (71 Lower Camden St., Dublin 2. Tel: (01-4760362) can order a long oak unit with open compartments and a leather seat on top. It costs €1700 and looks good enough to have in a hall. At the other end of the scale, **Jim Langan Furniture** (The Park, Carrickmines, County Dublin. Tel: 01-2943880) has an upright eight-drawer shoe storage box in glossy red or black for €50.

LIVING ROOM

The living area of Helen Kilmartin's Minima showroom on Herbert Place features the Wanda sofa by Premomoria, covered in velvet. This sofa costs €8700: you're paying for excellent quality and lasting style. The Middle-Eastern-style silk ceiling light is by Venetia Studium and costs €3356. The standard lamp to the left costs €1875. To the right are shelves by MDF Italia: price varies depending on size. Note the translucent curtaining covering not just the window opening but the whole wall.

SOFAS

'Superior construction is why some sofas are more expensive than others. They look better, feel more comfortable and will last longer. Choose a sofa with discreet legs: anything too obvious will date quickly. Also remember that a small sofa in a small room isn't going to give you a greater feeling of space. One long sofa is often better than a small couch and two armchairs: a single piece means less clutter.'

**Maria MacVeigh, interior designer
e-mail: mariamacveigh@ireland.com**

LOW PRICE

Buying a cheap sofa is never a good idea. It's a false economy. But if you *must*, you might as well go really low: The second-hand sofas at **Oxfam Home** (Francis Street, Dublin 8. Tel: 01-4020555 and Bray, County Wicklow. Tel: 01-2864173) look hideous – very old-fashioned fabrics and dated shapes. But they're cheap and tend to be quite clean and in reasonable order. They usually have sofas for €150 and three-piece suites for €175. If you buy one, you'll need to do something to smarten it up. For example, **KA International** (KA International (Main Street, Blackrock, County Dublin. Tel: 01-2782033 and Jervis Shopping Centre, Dublin 1. Tel: 01-8781052; branches also in Cork, Galway and Enniskerry; see www.kainternational.ie for details) has white cotton slip covers for about €200. They are made from one piece of adjustable cloth that fits over the whole sofa. These are among the best ready-made covers you can buy. Alternatively, have the sofa slip-covered properly, i.e. covers made to go over the body and the cushions together or separately. Slip-covered furniture can look sloppy, like a badly tailored dress, so be sure you and the person making it are in tune with the look you want. Husband and wife team **Muriel and Noel Rice** (Tel: 01-4935303); **Town & Country** in Cork (Tel: 021-4501468); and **Orla Carter** (Tel: 01-2980371) make slip covers to order. On the other hand, upholsterer **Paul Dempsey** (Tel: 087-6660064) can give an old couch a

Top left: a typical sofa by **O'Driscoll Furniture** – prices average €2900 depending on fabric.

Top right: the interior of an apartment in London by Irish interior designer **Orla Collins** (www.purple-design.com) – note how well a low sofa works in a tall room

Bottom left: Rudi and Nikki relax on a sofa made to order by **Merrion Square Interiors.**

Bottom right: a linen slip-covered sofa in the home of interior designer **Paul Austen**. The resin lamp by Marianna Kennedy (see lighting section in Around the House).

Top: Tess and Galen Bales of **www.w39.ie** are agents for top-end furniture lines. This is the living room of their apartment off Clanbrassil Street. They brought a sofa from their previous home in the US and had it copied by the **Sofa Factory**. It is covered in Andrew Martin fabric that matches the original.

Bottom left: silk cushions by **Helen James**, a textile designer better known for her scarves and wraps which are sold at Costume.

Bottom right: an L-shape sofa by **Living** in Bray. Something like this will cost about €3500.

facelift by restuffing it and recovering it in the traditional manner. This should cost about €350 for an average sofa. **Nick Summers** (Tel: 01-8256132) also comes recommended for this type of thing. Incidentally, you'll need about eight metres of fabric to cover an average sofa. Upholsterer **Joshua Duffy** (Tel: 01-4730390), an established father-and-son business on Francis Street, will transform a sofa. Known for their fine work, the Duffys will collect a sofa on Monday and return it on Friday of the same week, recovered and re-upholstered. A large piece may take a few days longer. Clients can supply fabric or choose from one of their sample books. Each sofa is different but, on average, the Duffys charge about €300 for labour and fabric will cost from €200 upwards. Someone who does something similar is Dermot Smyth of **Peach Tree Upholstery** in County Carlow (Tel: 059-9141624). He used to have a furniture shop and now just restores and upholsters. By all accounts, he's good and reasonably priced.

Have a pillow party. Try silk cushions by textile goddess Helen James. **Just go mad. To decide how many, ask yourself: if Prada made a garment from this fabric, would I buy it? Even one will make a statement. They cost between €80 and €125, through Bottom Drawer at** Brown Thomas **or** hjtextiles@eircom.net. **In any case, never buy cheap cushions. Good cushions can do a lot for a poor sofa and bad ones will drag down an expensive one. The cushions at** Eminence **(52 Sandycove Road, County Dublin. tel: 01-2300193; www.eminence. ie) are made from Asian fabrics and will soften a sofa with a hard line. Or try something by textile designer** Eva Kiernan **whose showroom (18 Kildare Street, Dublin 2. Tel: 01-6629553) is full of unusual things – see her leaf prints in particular.**

MID PRICE

At the lower end of the mid-price range, try **Famous Furniture** (Longmile Road, Dublin 12. Tel: 01-4050520). They sell cancelled orders and end-of-line stock from Laura Ashley, Marks & Spencer, Next, House of Fraser and even Harrods, all at half their original price. They operate on the basis that what you see on the floor can be bought and taken away the same day. Don't expect a fancy shop: this is a very unglamorous warehouse and your

first visit may not prove fruitful – there are lots of horrible sofas – but phone to ask which day new deliveries arrive, so you see the good stuff.

Few furniture shops have anything that can be bought and delivered a day or two later but **Diamond Living** (Longmile Road and Airside Retail Park, Swords. Tel: 1850-454444) tags sofas with an 'Express' sticker, indicating that they are in stock and available for immediate delivery. This a good place to find a straightforward fabric or leather sofa for about €1000. They usually have some nice 1950s-style leather sofas.

Duff Tisdall (537 North Circular Road, Dublin 1. Tel: 01-8558070 and Mill Street, Dublin 8. Tel: 01-4541355; www.duff-tisdall.ie) is an Irish company operated by designers Arthur Duff and Greg Tisdall. They design and make high-quality sofas that are contemporary but mercifully not overly of-the-moment. You'll get something great from about €2000 upwards.

Inreda (71 Lower Camden Street, Dublin 8. Tel: 01-4760362; www. inreda.ie) have sofas that will work with any room: quiet and unobtrusive, they are good for small spaces. Think neutral, timeless and think €2500 upwards.

Worth a look, too, is **O'Driscoll Furniture** (26-28 Lombard Street East, Dublin 2. Tel: 01-6711069; www.oddesign.ie): their sofas are a little quirky and large-scale, usually in great zingy colours. Also try Ligne Rosset at **Arnotts**: their sofas are less formal than others, with a lounge-around feel.

In Cork, go to **Bellissima** (Distillery Road, Bandon, County Cork. Tel: 023-54740; www.bellissima.ie), where owner Rosemary Jones has varied styles. In particular, have a look at her super-soft saddle-stitched Hermes-style leather couches for about €2500. **Marble & Lemon**, also in Cork (Emmet Place. Tel: 021-4271877) have more traditional, large American-style sofas, made locally. **Instore** in Limerick (061-416088 – branches also in Waterford and Galway) do the big comfortable slouchy couch well, often in velvet. **Mimosa Interiors** (Dún Laoghaire Shopping Centre. Tel: 01-2808166 and Cranford Centre, Montrose, Dublin

4. Tel: 01-2602443) do traditional comfortable styles but nothing too twee. I love their casual linen sofas: prices start at about €1700. They also do traditional leather button-back sofas in various dark colours.

There's always the **Sofa Factory** (Mill Street, Dublin 8. Tel: 01-4546877) but choose a good fabric. Other places to try for a mid-price contemporary sofa are **Bob Bushell** (Sir John Rogerson's Quay, Dublin 2. Tel: 01-671 0044; www.bobbushell.com); **European Living** (74b Kylemore Road, Dublin 10. Tel: 01-6269005); and **O'Hagan Design** (102 Capel street, Dublin 1. Tel: 01-8724016). For a traditional sofa try **Donaldson & Lyttle** (114 Lower George's Street, Dún Laoghaire. Tel: 01-2808454 and 11a Boucher Retail Park, Belfast. Tel: 028-90667333); **KA International**; and **Kilcroney Furniture** (Bray, County Wicklow. Tel: 01-2829361; www.kilcroneyfurniture.com). They usually have one or two things that are worthwhile. **Limited Edition** (96 Francis Street, Dublin 8. Tel: 01-4531123) have some art-deco-style sofas to order: always high on glamour.

Top: designer Arthur Duff on a sofa at his North Circular Road **Duff Tisdall** showroom.

Centre: sofas by **O'Driscoll Furniture** can be ordered in any colour, including this striking red

Bottom: a daybed by Natuzzi, an Italian company specialising in high-quality leathers and stocked by **Arnotts**. Try them for a contemporary sofa or armchair. They also offer pony-skin coverings and snakeskin coffee tables.

Centre: classic sofas
by Kingcome, pictured
here in soft tweed. They
can be ordered through
www.studio44.ie.

Bottom: **Brown
Thomas** has a range
of traditional leather
sofas and armchairs.
They are expensive but
very well finished.

If you want a traditional leather sofa,
don't overlook those at **Fired Earth** (31
Lower Ormond Quay, Dublin 1. Tel:
01-8735362 and 20 Lower George's
St, Dún Laoghaire, County Dublin.
Tel: 01-6636160). For example, the
Kid Glove chaise longue is available in
old-saddle brown or antiquated leather.
Prices start at €2496.

High end

There's a certain amount of crossover
between this section and the last – most
shops do a mix of mid and high prices.
However, in a contemporary style, the
'so-well-made-it-will-last-ten-years'
sofa can be found at **Minima** (8 Herbert
Place in Dublin 2. Tel: 01-6627894;
www.minima.ie) and **Haus** (Crow Street
and Pudding Row, Temple Bar, Dublin.
Tel: 01-6795155). Both sell sofas by
the best Italian companies such as Casa
Milano (at Minima) and B&B Italia (at
Haus). You're not going to get much
for less than €5000. My favourites at
the moment are those by Premomoria
at Minima (see the opening page of
this section). They are right on what's
happening in interiors but classic too:

light velvet fabrics, backs made up of several big cushions and deep seats. Also at **Minima,** look at Flexform sofas, designed by star designer Antonio Citterio: an L-shape with footstool costs €13,657. Why the high price? Few sofas are made to last as well.

A sofa I've lived with for the past year is the Canyon by **Orior** (12 Greenbank Industrial Estate, Newry, County Down. Tel: 028-30262620; www.oriorbydesign.com). Created by people who clearly have a soft spot for comfort, it's a sofa for hanging out on. It has one continuous deep-seat cushion and a row of separate cushions at the back. It can be ordered in many fabrics but I like it in linen with grey silk cushions. You can get an Orior sofa for about €3500 but realistically think €5000 plus.

Galleria (61 South William Street, Dublin 2. Tel: 01-6744736; branches in Cork and Galway) is another source for high-quality sofas…but be careful: the shop has horrors too.

Do try **Lomi** (Unit 124, Baldoyle Industrial Estate, Dublin 13. Tel: 01-8397001; www.lomi.ie). Most of their styles are quite architectural – i.e. a little hard-line – but still comfortable.

Brown Thomas (Grafton Street, Dublin 2. Tel: 01-6056666) is another good place: call and make an appointment to see the relevant salesperson who can explain everything. They have a few different manufacturers but the best is Italian company Meridiani. Just a couple of their sofas are on the floor (judge the quality) but a multitude of styles can be ordered, many quite different to anything else around. Prices range from €2000 to €6000.

On the traditional side I suggest **Minnie Peters** (56–7 Upper George's Street, Dún Laoghaire, County Dublin. Tel: 01-2805965) and **Helen Turkington (**47 Dunville Avenue, Ranelagh, Dublin 6. Tel: 01-4125138) – both specialise in big over-stuffed super-comfy sofas.

Almost all the shops mentioned already do sofa beds of some kind. Sorry, you're on your own – browse around! But try **Inreda** for a good range for contemporary styles, including single-bed sizes.

ARMCHAIRS

Above: actor Paul Congdon sits in a yellow chair by B&B Italia at **Haus**. This style is no longer available but is typical of the kind of showstopper piece you'll find at this shop.

Below left: a painted wicker armchair, like the one in this Dublin courtyard, can be found at **Wetherly's Furniture** in Deansgrange, wicker specialists.

Below right: actress Victoria Smurfit's dog Hercules perches on her Minotti armchair. Available at **Minima.**

Go to **Brown Thomas** for perfect versions of traditional leather armchairs; they look good from any angle, have a masculine presence and are evocative of 1940s country houses. The detailing is flawless. The Wessex chair, with antiqued leather, costs €1575 and is small but comfortable. The Chandler armchair is bigger and instead of a plain back, has a fluted effect. It costs €2225.

Interiors Bis (The Barn, Yeomanstown, Carragh, Naas, County Kildare. Tel: 045-856385; e-mail: interiorbis@ eircom.net) will make almost any style of armchair to order. I like their 1950-ish armless 'slipper' chairs. **Bygone Days** (The Cottage, Killashee, Naas, County Kildare. Tel: 045-901251) specialises in Victorian low-armed button-backed armchairs upholstered in a fabric of your choice.

It can be difficult to find a really comfy, traditional armchair. Performer Enda McGrattan suggests **Kilcroney Furniture** where he bought armchairs with 1930s-style curving sides: super-upholstered and very comfortable. 'It's not a place many people know but they have great armchairs.' You'll find something from about €300.

The best advice I can give someone looking for an armchair in a comfortable style that isn't attention-

grabbing or too cutting-edge, is to visit **KA International.** Have a look at the website (www.kainternational.ie) to see the multitude of styles that can be ordered: Georgian, Victorian, colonial and so on (think wingbacks and stretcher legs). You will also find some nice blocky 1930s- and 1950s-style armchairs, plus some very neutral contemporary versions. There are lovely armless bedroom chairs too. Each chair can be ordered in fabrics from the KA range: a lot of floral patterns but also lovely linens and plains. You'll need to spend from €450, depending on the chair and fabric chosen.

A lot of furniture inspires two responses: yawns and more yawns. Content by Conran, a line designed by Terence Conran and available at Arnotts doesn't look exciting at first glance but the range includes many nicely designed, adaptable pieces. How good they look depends on what you place them with. The aesthetic is very Conran, with plenty of oak. For example, an asymmetric bookshelf might cost €690; a side table with Scandinavian inspiration would be about €250; and upholstered pieces such as a chesterfield sofa with a deep seat are about €1900.

Top: French style armchair from **Homes In Heaven**. There are lots of variations, from €450.

Bottom: an example of the style of armchair you'll find at **Meadows & Byrne**. Prices usually start at about €300.

Far left: a tan leather Le Corbusier armchair costs €895 at **www.designclassicsdirect.ie**.

Left: a traditional nursing chair from **Bygone Days** can be ordered in any fabric. From €400.

RUGS

LOW PRICE

The **Renaissance** furniture store (114-116 Capel Street, Dublin 1. Tel: 01-8873809) is the place for inexpensive machine-made copies of Persian and other Oriental rugs. A 1.82 x 1.52m (6x5ft) rug sells for about €100. I've seen one used successfully in an apartment where colours are rich; it covers almost the entire living room floor, looking as if it cost more than its price tag. For contemporary rugs, **Plush Interiors** (Balllast Quay, Sligo. Tel: 071-9154912) has a good selection of wool-and-acrylic rugs (plain and with geometric patterns) that start at less than €200 for large sizes. **B&Q** (branches countrywide) is also worth a look for inexpensive rugs: for example, a 2.43 x 1.52m (8x5ft) good copy of a Persian-style rug costs €295 – it's acrylic, but you'd have to be down on your hands and knees to know. Check out the top floor at **Clerys** (O'Connell Street, Dublin. Tel: 01-8786000) for rugs. Occasionally you'll find a gem such as deep shag-pile wool rugs in natural colours for about €150 (they have some inexpensive carpets too, including flattened cord for €12 a square yard). As an alterative to a 'soft' rug, **Dwell** (M7 Business Park, Naas. Tel: 045-898134) has teak floormats made up of small pieces that cost about €200 for a large size. **Dunnes Home** (South Great George's Street,

Dublin 2, Cornelscourt, Dublin 18, and large Dunnes Stores branches countrywide) always has neutral rugs in stock, from €150.

Mid price

Start at **Habitat** (6-10 Suffolk Street, Dublin 2. Tel: 01-6771433; Fairgreen Road, Galway. Tel: 091-569980; and 41 Arthur Street, Belfast BT1 4GB. Tel: 028-90249522.) Their rug selection is reasonably broad and always features some unusual textures. If you like pastels and floral, **Laura Ashley** (Grafton Street, Dublin, Blanchardstown and Cork) usually has pretty traditional rugs.

There are few secrets left when it comes to finding well-priced quality in any area of home furnishings, but one is **Hollands** (St Patrick's Woollen Mills, Douglas, Cork. Tel 021-4898000). Although they sell contemporary designs, their authentic Oriental and Persian styles are exceptionally well-priced. For example, a Pakistan wool vegetable-dyed rug (6'6" x 5'2") might be a reasonable €1100. The colours are rich, the quality is excellent and everything is made in India and Pakistan under Fair Trade guidelines. Ask Dominique, the charming Frenchwoman who co-owns the store, about a line of contemporary rugs with graphic 1960-ish shapes, also made under ethical guidelines.

Try **Harriet's House** (60 Dawson Street, Dublin 2. Tel: 01-6777077 and 30 Blackrock Shopping Centre, County Dublin. Tel: 01-2884822) for thick faux-fur rugs in various colours, such as chocolate brown.

T**he Rug Gallery** (Coe's Road, Dundalk, County Louth. Tel: 042-9329851) is a good source for rugs that don't cost the earth. It's a bit hit and miss, though; sometimes they have nice things, sometimes not. **Duff Tisdall** has colourful heavily-textured rugs that could add fun and comfort to a severe, modernist setting (see picture opposite). Ligne Rosset at **Arnotts** (Henry Street, Dublin 1. Tel: 01-8050400) is also good for rugs, often with a quirky but subtle pattern. Large Aubusson-style rugs can be had from €450 at **Mimosa Interiors**.

HIGH END

Ceadogan Rugs (Wellington Bridge, County Wexford. Tel: 051-561349) will supply a hand-made rug or carpet to your specification – any shape, colour or pattern. Work with their design team to come up with something orginal. **Gillian Freedman** (01-6767782) makes wonderful hand-tufted rugs and woven tapestries to commission only. **Peter Linden** (George's Avenue, Blackrock. Tel: 01-2885875; www.peterlinden. com) is one of the best places to buy Persian and Chinese rugs and carpets in Dublin. These can be expensive: for example a 1930 11'6" x 8' Persian costs €13,500. However, their 'Dobag' collection starts at about €600. Now that Empires in the Westbury Mall has closed, a newcomer called **Oriental Rugs** (104 Francis Street, Dublin 8. Tel: 01-4531222) fills the void. It is

a veritable bazaar of colourful new, antique and semi-antique kilims, rugs and cushions, with prices ranging from a few hundreds to many thousands for the old. You can't beat the mellow tones of vegetable dyes and you should look for the characteristic 'abrash' rugs (where different hanks of wool have been used and where the change is obvious – it is considered a bonus). **Rug Art** (49 Sandycove Road, Sandycove, County Dublin. Tel: 01-2360126; www.rugart.ie) specialises in high-quality contemporary rugs and

has unusually textured pieces ranging in price. You can't do much more than walk on most rugs but a lot of theirs are so thick that you'll want to sit and lie on them too. Rug Art is all about low-key luxury and has the most covetable rugs around.

MIRRORS

Most homes need a few large mirrors and the cheapest way to get them in whatever size you fancy is from **Myra Glass** (New Street, Dublin 8. Tel: 01-4533321). For example, a 4ft-square

Left: a mirror from **Meadows & Byrne**. They usually have a good selection of standard mirrors. Also in Dún Laoghaire, try **Inside Out** (97 Lower George's Street, County Dublin. Tel: 01-2148685) for something rather straightforward.

Right: carved, painted and distressed mirrors from **Minnie Peters**.

35

Oak-top coffee table with vintage finish and iron legs, from €1150 at the **Enniskerry Trading Company** in County Wicklow. Tel: 01- 2866275. Go to this shop for high-quality traditional coffee tables with a relaxed feel.

Centre: a coffee table from **Meadows & Byrne**. This is typical of their practical tables – they almost always have something with more than one shelf underneath.

Bottom: a glass coffee table has obvious space-expanding advantages in a small room. Try **Mobilia** for a selection of sizes to order.

bevelled mirror with holes drilled for wall mounting costs about €130.

As well as some mock-gilt horrors, **B&Q** always has inexpensive mirrors in simple frames in big sizes. Ditto **Dunnes Home**. Something more decorative can be found at **Laura Ashley** – plenty of 1930s styles – and **Yesterday Once More** (3 Carysfort Avenue, Blackrock, County Dublin. Tel: 01-2108410) which has Venetian styles from €250 in heart and oval shapes. **Harriet's House** has mirrors from about €300 and sizes suitable for over a mantelpiece: imagine mirrors with trellis trompe l'oeil effects, padded snakeskin, painted carved wood and black gilt reproduction Regency styles. **Baggot Framing Gallery** (13 Eastmoreland Place, Dublin 4. Tel: 01-6606063) will supply mirrors in a variety of frames. For something completely different, go to furniture designer **Kate Fine** (Tel: 01-670369; www.finedesign.ie) who specialises in mirrors. Her 'bar code' design (framed in leather and wall-mounted in various configurations) is one of her most popular pieces. The **Dalkey Design**

Company (20 Railway Road, Dalkey, County Dublin. Tel: 01-2856827) always has large-scale painted or gilded mirrors, often antique. Jeweller **John Farrington** (32 Drury Street, Dublin 2. Tel: 01-6791899) has a storeroom next to his shop that's stocked with large new and antique gilt over-mantel mirrors.

COFFEE TABLES

Before you buy, consider:
Height – who doesn't eat the odd meal in front of the TV?
Weight: will you want to move your table frequently?
Safety: table corners should never be razor-sharp.

LOW PRICE

Dunnes Home is a good start. Stock changes frequently. Go really low and look at the **Argos** catalogue (branches countrywide) but choose something non-identifiable, such as their standard black glass-and-metal table for €99.99.

Instore (Limerick, Tel: 061-416088; Waterford, Tel: 051-844882; Galway, Tel: 091-530085 and Sligo, Tel: 071-

9149174) always has a white New England-ish criss-cross-legged table for €199 (square) or €189 (rectangular). At **Touchwood** (35 Hamilton Street, South Circular Road, Dublin 8. Tel: 01-4539711) you will find low, rustic, country-style tables.

MID PRICE

Habitat coffee tables are good for a first-time buyer but **Living** (South William Street, Dublin 2. Tel: 01-6751898; and Castle Street, Bray, County Wicklow. Tel: 01-2828905) is the place for a coffee table that won't cost more than about €400, while **Inreda** has low-key high-quality modern tables from companies you'll find at the Milan Furniture Fair – there's always something interesting there. **Furnishing Distributors** (7 Bray South Business Park, Killarney Rd, Bray, County Wicklow. Tel: 01-2765811) can order Andrew Martin coffee tables (www.andrewmartin.com) and have a few on display. On the website see big low square coffee tables that can be used to display photographs and objects. See also a Thai teak style, a

Above left: Helen McAlinden's papier mâché coffee table once sat in Sybil Connolly's home. **O'Sullivan Antiques** will source something similar, at a price.

Centre: this Minotti table with onyx marble top can be ordered from **Minima** for €2724.

Right: the Garouste & Bonetto table is a collector's piece.

Below: a large low coffee table in wenge, typical of what you'll find at **Instore**.

zinc-panelled beech table, an iron table with slat base and a chrome scissor-legged table with leather tray top. **Eminence** has Asian tables suitable for use as coffee tables that will bring character to a contemporary room. All the shops mentioned already in this section do coffee tables but take a trip to Dún Laoghaire first. Visit the **Collection** (Unit 4, St Helen's Court, Lower George's Street, Dún Laoghaire, County Dublin. Tel: 01-2147700), **Fired Earth, Meadows & Byrne** (The Pavilion, Royal Marine Road, Dún Laoghaire, County Dublin. Tel: 01-2804554), **Minnie Peters** and **Homes in Heaven** (3 Anglesea Buildings, George's Street, Dún Laoghaire, County Dublin. Tel: 01-2802077).

HIGH END

Elizabeth Garouste and Mattia Bonetti's round polished stainless-steel coffee table stands out and fades away at the same time. It's a collector's dream. The twenty-year-old partnership between these two designers is celebrated and if a piece of contemporary furniture can hold its value this is it. It costs from £20,000. The agent here is interior designer **Sirin Lewendon** (sirin@sirinlewendon.com). Minotti at **Haus** and **Minima** has some of the best, dateless modern coffee tables – mostly in large sizes.

Ligne Rosset at **Arnotts** is good for large low tables. But be aware that some cost a lot of money (€1200 plus) for items that a good handyman could put together. Try **Rua** (1 Lower George's Street, Dún Laoghaire, County Dublin. Tel: 01-2304209) for tables designed by Tom O'Rahilly. Everything he does is original and understated and will add elegance to a room. Pieces with unusual veneers are precious tables

with prices to match – over €1500. Or commission a table from **Lorraine Brennan** (Tel: 01-8735420; www. fiftyeightb.ie). She'll make something low-key but perfect. See the Special section for style-specific coffee tables.

SCREENS

Use screens to soften a corner, hide a computer desk or divide a room. Here are just two ideas for something special:

Arroo in County Leitrim (Tel: 071-9856997; www.arroo.ie) design and hand-make pretty painted screens. All the designs can be ordered in different colours (see the website). The chrysanthemum screen pictured here is inspired by Chinese embroidery. Each panel costs €175 and measures 182cm x 52cm.

On a more contemporary note, pictured here is furniture designer **Gregor Timlin** (www.gregortimlin. com), who makes screens to order. Also try **Brown Thomas**, **Habitat** and smaller shops such as the **Collection** and **Helen Turkington**.

Top left: designer **Gregor Timlin** with his folding screen.

Bottom left: Use a painted screen by **Arroo** to divide a multi-function room.

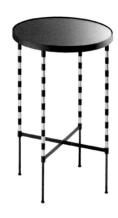

Side tables

Think outside the box. Side tables
can be a room's quirky accent. Try
dealers on Francis Street for antique
chests (or check out auctions for
lower price tags). **Eminence** has lovely
Chinese-style drums that can be used
as a resting spot for a drink or a book.
Designer **Leo Scarff** (see www.jist.ie)
does a little table that's low but handy:
a tray on a tripod base, it costs just
€55. **Flanagans Of Buncrana** (Deerpark
Road, Mount Merrion.Tel: 01-2880218)
have many styles of small authentic-
looking reproduction tables. **Thornby
Hall** (Naas, County Kildare. Tel: 045-
9015511), located down a winding
laneway, is a warehouse-type space
crammed with reproduction furniture
in French and English styles. It's a
good hunting ground for affordable
side tables – wrought iron or marble-
topped, with plenty of carved wood.

Nests of tables

My favourite is House of Fraser's stained oak set (Dundrum Town Centre Dublin 14. Tel: 01-2991400). It costs €469 and can also be ordered from **House of Ireland** (37 Nassau Street, Dublin 2. Tel: 01-6711111). Nordic Living (57 Main Street, Blackrock, County Dublin. Tel: 01-2886680)) have perfect Alvar Aalto nests from €700: timeless and beautifully made. For something inexpensive I'd go first to **Dunnes Home** – you'll get a simple veneered nest for about €100. Try **Vobe Interiors** (Carrick-on-Shannon, County Leitrim and Ballinalack, County Westmeath; see www.vobeinteriors. ie) for rustic styles from €300. **Marks & Spencer**'s furniture department in Mary Street in Dublin usually has a few basic nests from about €350. Also try **Arnotts**; between Ligne Rosset and Sherry Furniture, you're likely to find something.

Right: a nest of tables from **House of Fraser**. Also available in natural oak. Kiki wears a vintage Antonia Campbell Hughes dress.

Dining Room

Sonia Reynolds at home in her combined kitchen and dining area. The teak table and chairs were bought from Olivia Delaney at 20th-Century Furniture, a concession in Habitat, Dublin. This is typical of what you'll find there: it's late 1950s Scandinavian Modern. Three leaves change the shape from circular to oval. Similar tables cost from €1500.

TABLES

'A dining table brings people together, so it should be inviting to sit at. I like this oval walnut table (above) by John Hutton for Ensemble. It has a chunky top, a beautiful base and is available through **Milo Fitzgerald Interiors**, Lavistown, County Kilkenny (Tel: 056-7771306) – a snip at €8500!'

Sarah Cruise, interior designer
e-mail: sarah@designintervention.ie

There are plenty of dining 'sets' (table and chairs together) and many of the shops in this section sell them. However I'm in favour of a non-matching dining table and chairs: they make for a more interesting room. That doesn't have to mean a dramatic contrast – just avoid anything too co-ordinated.

Measurements alone don't make it easy to visualise how much space a dining table will take up. Take the dimensions of whatever you have your eye on and use them to create a 'shadow' of the piece from old newspapers. All you need are scissors, sticky-tape and patience. Position the taped-together newspapers where the table will sit to get an idea of the effect on your floor space.

Whether your dining area is a separate room or part of an open-plan living space, below are a few ideas. Most of these shops do large or small sizes and folding or dropleaf tables.

LOW PRICE
You've moved into your first home. Its combined living and dining area might be small and you don't have the bona fide furniture – or budget – to fill it straight away. Still you want to entertain friends with a modicum of style. To make a cheap, sturdy dining table, buy two trestles from **Habitat** (6-10 Suffolk Street, Dublin 2. Tel: 01-6771433; Fairgreen Road, Galway. Tel: 091-569980; and 41 Arthur Street, Belfast BT1 4GB. Tel: 028-90249522.) at €75 each. Then go to **Woodworkers**

Clockwise from top left: interior designer **Paul Austen** used a trestle table with an MDF top in his Drumcondra kitchen/dining area; everyone needs an object whose only point is to be pleasing – indulge yourself with a glass platter by artist **Eva Kelly** (Tel: 045-485389); **www.designclassicsdirect.com** sell this marble-topped Eero Saarinen table and Hans Wagner wishbone chair; an inexpensive table and chairs from **Habitat**, always good for small tables and stackable chairs.

(1–10 Mount Tallant Avenue, Dublin 6w. Tel: 01-4901968): they will cut a sheet of MDF to whatever size you need from about €30. Finally, have the MDF painted high gloss or throw some fabric across the whole thing. Interior designer Paul Austen created a very simple table in this way (see previous page). Instead of trestles, you could use old office tables that can sometimes be picked up at shops such as **Christy Bird** (32 Richmond Street South, Dublin 2. Tel: 01-4750409). For a cheap flatpack table, try **Argos** (branches countrywide): their oak-veneered dining tables cost about €200 and are unremarkable but inoffensive. **Dunnes Home** (South Great George's Street, Dublin 2, Cornelscourt, Dublin 18, and large Dunnes Stores branches countrywide) is an obvious place to pick up a plain timber dining table for a couple of hundred euro. **Muji** (5 Chatham St, Dublin 2. Tel: 01-6794591) always has a small table for €650 with a nice roughness to its surface. It has drop leaves and is probably best for an apartment or small kitchen. Matching chairs are €149

each. **Marks & Spencer**'s perennial 'Nevada' glass-top table has 'X' shape oak legs and costs €549 – but paint the legs black and it will be far more chic. Also see the note on auctions in the Around the House section: you'll pick up something solid and inexpensive, but usually rather rustic.

MID PRICE

Eero Saarinen's round table with white and grey marble top was designed in the 1960s and reproductions from about €1400 can be ordered through **Mobilia** (Drury Hall, Lower Stephen's Street, Dublin 2. Tel: 01-4780177), **Sienna Design** (29 Patrick Street, Kilkenny. Tel: 056-7790771) and **Brown Thomas** (Grafton Street, Dublin 2. Tel: 01-6056666). It doesn't take up much space but can seat six people and is good for a small apartment where you won't want anything too heavy looking. You can put almost any type of chair with it. The designer was one of the first to do a 'trumpet' shape because he wanted to get rid of the chaos around the base of a table – there's always a mass of chair legs. For other round tables, **Habitat** always has a few, also with small pedestal bases. Expect to pay about €400. Round wooden tables can usually be found at **Diamond Living** (Longmile Road and Airside Retail Park, Swords. Tel: 1850-454444). For a sturdy chunk of a table try **Marble & Lemon** (Emmet Place, Cork. Tel: 021-4271877). They almost always have solid walnut tables which can comfortably seat ten people and cost about €1200. For small spaces, **Living** (South William Street, Dublin 2. Tel: 01-2828905 and Castle Street, Bray. Tel: 01-2828905) usually have simple circular high-gloss tables (I like them white) for about €500.

An extendable table with removable leaves provides extra flexibility to accommodate parties of different sizes. Sherry Furniture's Rossmore range at **Arnotts** (Henry St, Dublin 1. Tel: 01-8050400) specialises in extendable dark-wood colonial-style drawleaf tables. A dropleaf table is an obvious choice if you want something that can be folded down and pushed to one side of the room. For antique versions browse Francis Street. But if you want a new one (in an antique style) try **Traditional Designs** (Bushfield Avenue, off Marlborough Road, Dublin 4. Tel: 01-4126055). This shop has a good and reasonably authentic-looking range of

Left: in her Rathmines home, interior designer Deirdre Whelan mixes an antique table with chairs by Cassina from **Haus**. The adjustable lamp behind is by Artemide, an Italian company, and is available at **Bob Bushell**.

Centre: create the mood with napkin holders from **Brown Thomas**.

Right: this table and chairs are the kind of thing you'll find at **Bellissima**.

reproduction furniture, including lots
of dining tables. **Robert Scott Designs**
(59 Capel Street, Dublin 1. Tel: 01-
8740654; www.robertscottdesigns.
com) is a good place to find a basic,
straightforward rectangular table,
usually in oak or wenge veneer. You'll
get something big and solid for about
€400: not terribly exciting but it means
you can put money into buying high-
quality or unusual chairs elsewhere.
For an extendable pale-painted table in
a Swedish or New England style from

about €1000 or for a dark-wood table,
try **Mimosa Interiors** (Dún Laoghaire
Shopping Centre. Tel: 01-2808166
and Cranford Centre, Montrose,
Dublin 4. Tel: 01-2602443). **Jennifer
Goh** (Landmark Court, Carrick-on-
Shannon, County Leitrim. Tel: 071-
9622208. www.jennifergohdesign.
com) specialises in Asian antiques
and should be able to source any size
you need. Try the **Antique Warehouse**
(www.theantiquewarehouse.ie) for
original French 1930s art deco dining

tables and chairs, at prices that aren't stratospheric. There are always shops such as **Classic Furniture** (The Park, Carrickmines, County Dublin. Tel: 01-2076566; for other branches see www.classicfurniture.ie) if you want something straightforward that won't cost the earth. With such a table, it's all about the chairs you use and how you decorate the rest of the room. See the Kitchen section for breakfast tables that can also be used as small dining tables.

Also try: **Square Deal Interiors** (Washington Street, Cork. Tel: 021-4274045) for basic Italian dining sets – choose the simplest you can find; **Furniture Designs** (Old Bawn Road, Tallaght, Dublin 24. Tel: 01-4515326) for decent tables for a couple of hundred euro. **Instore** (Limerick, Tel: 061-416088; Waterford, Tel: 051-844882; Galway, Tel: 091-530085 and Sligo, Tel: 071-9149174) always has a very broad offering at fairly reasonable prices. Try **House of Fraser** (Dundrum Town Centre Dublin 14. Tel: 01-2991400) too: they have a small selection of contemporary tables. At **Brown Thomas** (Grafton Street, Dublin 2. Tel: 01-6056666) you see one or two well-selected dining tables – look towards the back end of the third floor.

Antique linen can provide a lovely contrast to a contemporary dining table. Enriqueta MacVeigh **(085-7186022) sells beautiful table linen at the farmers' market in Leopardstown, County Dublin on Fridays and at Castlebellingham, County Louth on Sundays. At** Jenny Vander **(50 Drury Street, Dublin 2. Tel: 01-6770406) you will find embroidered lace tablecloths from €90–€240. Go along to events organised by** Antiques Fairs Ireland **(Tel: 087-2670607 www.antiquesfairsireland.com) where Della Bagnel shows table and bed linen.**

High End

Maxalto's dining tables (prepare to spend at least €4000) at **Haus** (Crow Street/Pudding Row, Temple Bar, Dublin. Tel: 01-6795155; www. haus.ie), will be at home in any environment and will stay discreetly beautiful forever. They have a high level of luxury but remain true to the material (often open-pore stained oak). Haus has wonderful stuff (although be prepared for longish delivery times): B&B Italia's dining tables are always perfection. I love the restraint of their

Above: the ubiquitous Balloon chair from **Bob Bushell**.

Top right: Saarinen table and leather chairs from **Minima**.

Bottom right: red oak table and chairs by **O'Driscoll Furniture**.

Far right, from top: chairs from **SKI Interiors**; **Homes In Heaven**; and **Helen Turkington**.

glass-topped tables: you get style with the volume turned down. Again they cost from about €4000. If you're trailing around looking for a dining table that exists only in your head, try **Habitat**'s Dublin shop, which is an access-point for esteemed Irish furniture designer **Charles O'Toole** (www.charlesfurniture.ie). He has a service called 'One-Off', which means he will work with you to create a piece of furniture that will fit your taste, room and budget. Within reason, though: you've got to spend a little money to create something special. And think modern. Initial enquiries and meetings are free, but there is a €150 charge for secondary concepts and drawings, which is refundable when the order goes ahead. Also at Habitat in Dublin, try **20th-Century Furniture**, a concession within the store (see photograph on the opening page of this section). They always have a few beautiful solid wood tables in stock, if not always on the shop floor. See the Antiques section and the Special section for more ideas: almost all the shops listed sell dining tables in the style of the shop. Also try **Lomi** (Unit 124, Baldoyle Industrial Estate, Dublin 13. Tel: 01-8397001; www.lomi.ie) – for elegant modern tables; **Casey's Furniture** (65 Oliver Plunkett Street, Cork. Tel: 021-4270393; and Raheen, Limerick. Tel: 061-307070) for tables by Ligne Rosset.

Be a label queen. Get the Hermès silver chopsticks for €135 at Brown Thomas. **They'll give you a shiver every time you order in. The sushi tray is €76. Whatever you do, don't buy a set of dishes: vulgar!**

CHAIRS

A chair needs to be good-looking as well as functional: when not in use, it's most often seen from behind. Examine potential candidates from all sides. If you opt for an upholstered look, steer clear of delicate fabrics.

'Dining chairs are always one of the last things we supply because good ones are so hard to find. More often than not, I get them made up to my design. A dining chair should be a marriage of comfort and aesthetics. It's one of the few pieces of furniture – along with your bed and sofa – that must be comfortable.'

Helen Roden, interior designer
www.merrionsquareinteriors.com

LOW PRICE

Go to one of the sales held every Thursday at 10 am at **Herman Wilkinson**'s auction rooms in Rathmines, Dublin 6 (01-4972245). You'll find old wood chairs with plenty of 'character' selling cheaply. You're not going to get a Georgian stretcher. Sharon Dunne of the **Linen Berry** (Geraldine Court, Maynooth, County Kildare. Tel: 01-6293094) suggests an easy way to rejuvenate basic chairs: 'Invest in a staple gun and recover

Above: chair by **Ensemble**.

Below: chair from **Habitat**.

them yourself. Most ordinary chairs have seats that can be unscrewed. Cover the seat with your new fabric, using the staple gun to secure it, then rescrew the seat. You should only need a metre and a half of fabric to do six chairs.' Dunne has good quality fabrics from €25 a metre.

The Balloon dining chair (see page 50) costs about €100 and can be ordered through **Bob Bushell** (1-2 Sir John Rogerson's Quay, Dublin 2. Tel: 01-6710044). A Scandinavian/Alvar Aalto influence takes this chair beyond fashion...but classics can be boring so use it in an imaginative way (i.e. not with a bland wood floor and white walls). For a very small apartment, buy folding chairs so you can push them against a wall and create more floor space. **Habitat** always has a nice selection.

As mentioned in the Living Room section, **Famous Furniture** (Longmile Road, Dublin 12. Tel: 01-4050520) is a warehouse that sells discounted stock from mainstream shops – it's a bit hit and miss but worth exploring. All in all though, a decent inexpensive chair is hard to find so try to spend a little more – good chairs have a long lifespan.

MID PRICE

Look beyond domestic furniture shops: the Eiffel Tower dining chair by Vitra, designed in the 1960s by Charles Eames, costs €180 at **Project Office** (2 Exchange Street Upper, Dublin 8. Tel: 01-6715700). 'I have this in my own home and it's very comfortable,' says interior designer Robert Trench. 'It works with many different tables and can be ordered in lots of colours.' Vitra are the manufacturers of many a mid-20th-century classic chair.

In a traditional vein, Sherry Furniture's Rossmore line at **Arnotts** does styles such as ladder-back chairs and a nicely finished seagrass chair (you wouldn't dine on this chair, you'd *eat* – it's a good kitchen chair). There are button-back upholstered dining chairs at **Mimosa Interiors**. The Louis Ghost chair by Philippe Starck costs €150 at **Urban Outfitters** (4 Cecilia St, Dublin 2. Tel: 01-6706202) and is very identifiable but still a great chair (a retro shape in a moulded plastic) that can be placed with a variety of tables. Mix around a table in different coloured tints. At **Renaissance Interiors** (Stone Manor House, Naas Road, Rathcoole, County Dublin. Tel: 01-4587373). you'll find every style of reproduction dining chair (mostly to order) including some upholstered ones that are practically armchairs. If you are looking for a contemporary dining chair, **2cooldesign** (Cow's Lane, Temple Bar. Dublin 8. Tel: 01-6725402; info@2cooldesign.ie) has a huge selection available.

HIGH PRICE

Given the interminable nature of Irish dinner parties, a comfortable chair is essential. German furniture company Ensemble and their designer John Hutton excel at comfy seating for those to whom money is no object: dining chairs start at a whopping €1700 for a side chair and rise to €3000 for a leather chair! They are often inspired by art deco and 1950s styles and are rather beautiful. The back and seat are always well proportioned: important for comfort. Contact Irish agent **Milo**

Fitzgerald (Tel: 056-7771306) and see a selection at his showroom outside Kilkenny. One of **O'Driscoll Furniture**'s staple pieces is a beautifully understated red oak timber chair for €325 (pictured on page 51). It's robust and would sit around a table without screaming its presence. It is available with or without a leather-padded seat. At **Helen Turkington** (Dunville Avenue, Ranelagh, Dublin 6. Tel: 01-4125138) ask about the Dining Chair Company (www.diningchair.co.uk) for some elegant, romantic 1930s styles – most are upholstered. You will also find well-made upholstered chairs from €350 at **Minnie Peters** (56 Upper George's Street, Dún Laoghaire. Tel: 01-2805965). But steer away from anything that looks like a hotel chair. In a more contemporary vein, the Cab chair (encased in leather) designed by Mario Bellini for Cassina is considered to be a modern classic. Ask about it at **Nordic Living** (57 Main Street, Blackrock, County Dublin. Tel: 01-2886680). Another timeless dining seat is the Wishbone chair designed by Hans J. Wegner in 1950.

Chairs by Sherry Furniture at **Arnotts**.

DINING ROOM

53

Left: you'll find chairs like these at **Living** in Bray.

Centre: **Minnie Peters** has French-style painted sideboards.

Right: a Zebrano sideboard by **O'Driscoll Furniture**.

Inspired by classical portraits of Danish merchants sitting in Ming chairs, the Wishbone chair is crafted by the original manufacturer, Carl Hansen & Son, from steam-bent, oil-treated oak with a woven black cord seat. It's more comfortable than it looks and is available from €500 at **www.designclassicsdirect.com**.

SIDEBOARDS

Find sideboards with a retro influence such as the zebrano wood version (below) for about €1800 at **O'Driscoll Furniture**. At **Limited Edition** (96 Francis Street, Dublin 8. Tel: 01-4531123) glamorous art deco style sideboards have fluted columns and can be ordered in different woods, some with a lacquered finish, others matt. They cost about €3000. The **Collection** (Unit 4, St Helen's Court, Lower George's Street, Dún Laoghaire, County Dublin. Tel: 01-2147700) usually has a few deep console tables in unusual woods or leather finishes that could be used as sideboards. At **20th-Century Furniture** in **Habitat** find 1950s Scandinavian sideboards and the occasional piece from earlier periods. At a very different price level and style, the main floor at Habitat is worth exploring for 'fade-away' sideboards – for example, black-stained oak

pieces with press-and-release doors and handles. **Peter Johnson Interiors** on Cow's Lane (Temple Bar, Dublin 2. Tel: 01-6334325) always has one special sideboard. Also visit **Retrospect** next door (01-6726188) – again, you'll find just one or two great things. The Carrickmines branch of **Classic Furniture** (The Park, Dublin 18. Tel: 01-2076566) is not the most glamorous place but upstairs are some really great long glossy drawer cabinets for around €1200. These are technically bedroom pieces but I think they're suitable for a dining room too.

Secondary pieces of furniture can provide an opportunity to add character to your dining room. Look at places such as **Villa and Hut** (79 Main Street, Gorey, County Wexford. Tel: 053-9481162 and Unit 12A, St. Patrick's Mills, Douglas, County Cork. Tel: 021-4367792) for hardwood Indonesian sideboards (all from fair-trade sources). They're a little rough around the edges, a nice contrast to a slick dining table. Also try **Crystal & Silk** (1 Michael Street, Wexford. Tel: 053-9144203) – for reproduction dark-wood and pale painted pieces; **Arnotts**; and **Houseworks** (11-15 Upper Erne Street, Dublin 2. Tel: 01-6769511; www.houseworks.ie) for contemporary mid-price sideboards.

Left: The Cab dining chairs in this room are by Cassina from **Haus** – similar Egg chairs can be ordered from **Living**.

Right: Multi-drawer white lacquered sideboard from **McNally Living**. Their showroom has a full selection of dining-room furniture, priced from mid to high end.

KITCHEN

Bob Crowley's kitchen in London. Cork-born Crowley is a Tony-Award-winning set designer. His kitchen was made by a carpenter using simple flush presses and is painted a dark shade of grey: sometimes there's no need to spend a lot of money on kitchen units.

'**Lomi** is a showroom in the Baldoyle Industrial Estate full of beautiful high-end contemporary furniture (Tel: 01-8397001; www.lomi.ie) and they also do some wonderful kitchens. I like those by Santos (www.santos.ie), a Spanish company I saw first at the Interior Design Show at the RDS. The look is very streamlined and elegant in a modern way. Plus they are so well made – even inside the compartments – but not as expensive as other kitchens. Lomi are really easy to deal with – always reliable.'

Michela Mantero, interior designer
e-mail: michelamantero@eircom.net

KITCHENS

LOW PRICE

If you're looking for something different from the standard kitchen, you're in luck. Cabinetmakers have never been as eager to provide a kitchen that suits your style and needs. Spending a huge amount of money on a kitchen isn't always necessary. **Alan Gallagher** (Tel: 087-2265362) can make simple units that could end up looking better and costing less than other options. He'll design something around your budget (MDF, timber or melamine), make it and install it himself. He is a pleasant guy and I haven't come across a client who doesn't praise his work, including Emma Kelly of Elevate PR, who used him to make various units for her home. Journalist Aoife Tunney's traditional kitchen timber units were built by cabinetmaker **Roland Henderson** (Tel: 086-2642743) whose clients also include Bono. For any kind of joinery interior designer Michela Mantero recommends **KCR Joinery** (Lower Kimmage Road, Dublin 6w. Tel: 01-4067672) for good finish and reasonable prices. Interior designer Clodagh Conroy suggests the **Panelling Centre** (109 Longmile Rd, Walkinstown, Dublin 12. Tel: 01-4564899 and Sallynoggin Road. Tel: 01-2849988) if you don't have a lot to spend. 'You'll get a galley kitchen for about €3500,' she says. This is the ready-to-wear of kitchen cabinets; frugal buyers can enhance economy cabinets with details such as handles

Clockwise from top left: Denise Fitzpatrick's kitchen in County Meath features an Aga and units by **Minnie Peters**; journalist Aoife Tunney's kitchen was made by **Roland Henderson**; delph at **Dunnes Home**; this Sandycove, County Dublin, kitchen was supplied by **Kitchen Flair** in Sandymount, Dublin; **Designwood** in Rathmines, Dublin, made this painted kitchen; Frances O'Gorman (owner of the Cherche Midi shoe shop) with her son Shane in their kitchen made by the **Panelling Centre**. 'It's a great place to get a smart-looking kitchen that doesn't cost a lot. I used an expensive grey marble countertop and good handles to give it a feel of luxury,' says Frances.

Top: a kitchen supplied by **Shannonside Kitchens** for a house in Blackrock, County Dublin.

Bottom: a model by **Snaidero Kitchens** on Drury Street.

or countertops, and elements such as pull-out recycling bins.

Ikea (www.ikea.com) is a good source for taps, sink and countertops that don't cost the earth. Many people have started to buy flat-pack kitchens from Ikea and have a joiner fit them here. Take a cheap flight to Prestwick and visit the Glasgow branch (the only one with a delivery service to Ireland). Look in particular for the Udden freestanding units (see website): chic and affordable. Elements of some **B&Q** (nationwide) kitchens are not bad either. Go to **Habitat** (6-10 Suffolk Street, Dublin 2. Tel: 01-6771433; Fairgreen Road, Galway. Tel: 091-569980; and 41 Arthur Street, Belfast BT1 4GB. Tel: 028-90249522) for modular freestanding kitchen units. At **Cash & Carry Kitchens** (nine showrooms in Dublin, Cork, Limerick and Galway; see www.cashandcarrykitchens.com) you'll get a basic kitchen. The **Dún Laoghaire Kitchen Centre** (8 Cumberland Street, Dún Laoghaire, County Dublin. Tel: 01-2300336; www.dunlaoghairekitchencentre.ie) has a

showroom with fifteen fitted kitchens on display which cost from €4000. They are best for the painted look. They also supply appliances by Siemens, Zanussi, Waterford Stanley, Fisher & Paykel and Aga.

A good furniture buy isn't only about price; it's also about flexibility. A butcher's trolley from Dunnes Home (**South Great George's Street, Dublin 2, Cornelscourt, Dublin 18, and large Dunnes Stores branches nationwide**) provides extra counter space for a small kitchen. 'Kitchens in most apartments tend to be small so a butcher's trolley from Dunnes creates extra work space if you've an open plan layout,' says Tracy Tucker, owner of Costume boutique, who bought a trolley. 'It means two people can prepare food at the same time. There are two wire drawers beneath a solid top so you get more storage too – they're good for holding large serving dishes.' Butchers' trolleys start at €175.

MID PRICE

Look beyond Dublin! **Shannonside Kitchens** (St Nessans Road, Dooradoyle Limerick. Tel: 061-228937) made the painted New England-style kitchen pictured opposite at a lower price than it might have cost from a Dublin supplier. **Delgrey Kitchens** (Kilcoole,

County Wicklow. Tel: 01-2871072; www.delgrey.ie) supplied the kitchen in Rathgar (see next page) which cost about €22,000.

Houseworks (11-15 Upper Erne Street, Dublin 2. Tel: 01-6769511; branches in Dublin, Cork & Belfast, see www.houseworks.ie for details) deal with Siematic kitchens, which cost from €16,000 and are available freestanding, fully fitted or modular. They also stock the top brands – Neff, Bosch, Gaggenau, De Dietrich. At mid-price level also try: **Dundrum Kitchens** (Apollo Building, Dundrum Road, Dublin. Tel: 01-2898709) and **Danish Design (**69 Main Street, Blackrock, County Dublin. Tel: 01-2789040).

For a homely, country-style kitchen, **Fired Earth** (31 Lower Ormond Quay, Dublin 1. Tel: 01-8735362 and 20 Lower George's St, Dún Laoghaire, County Dublin. Tel: 01-6636160) isn't as expensive as you might imagine: their Shaker-style range prices, including sinks and taps, start at €10,910 for the small galley kitchen, €14,292 for the family kitchen and €25,018 for the large living kitchen.

Above: a kitchen
by **Delgrey** in
County Wicklow.

Shaker-style sideboards cost about €1200, kitchen tables start at €1300 and ladder-back chairs with woven seats cost about €200. The collection is available in seven colours including strong greens and deep pinks. Still popular is the Bastide kitchen range with its quintessential French country look. Accompanying Belfast sinks cost €287.

For a painted fitted kitchen here are a few places to try: the **Tipperary Furniture Company** (Clonoulty, Cashel, County Tipperary. Tel: 0504-42493; www.tipperaryfurniture.com). If you like a pale look with pine handles and timber worktops – along with the obligatory Belfast sink. Also try **Hogan Kitchens** (Beechmount Industrial Estate, Navan, County Meath. Tel: 046-9022374; www.hogankitchens. com) who do a particular kind of kitchen better than most, more subtle and authentic. Their kitchens, which generally start at about €18,000, have real New England personality and they do all the usual top appliances. In Cork, try **Coach House Kitchens** (Carhue, Coachford, County Cork. Tel: 021-7334098; www.coach-house-kitchens.com). Their traditional styles are more authentic than twee and they also make fitted units for studies, bathrooms and bedrooms. Ditto the **Victorian Salvage & Joinery Company**, (South Glouchester Street, Dublin 2. Tel: 01-6727000), who make solid wood freestanding and fitted kitchens from new or salvaged oak, maple or pitch-pine. For a hand-made wood kitchen, sometimes it's better to go to a small company: for example, **Joe Vaughan Kitchens** (Bellinter, Navan, County Meath. Tel: 086-8970219) and **Peter McKiernan** (Tel: 01-2011901; 087-2436150).

HIGH END

This category represents the couture end of the kitchen cabinet spectrum. What you want is what you get – and you pay for it. If you have specific needs and deep pockets, one of these suppliers could be the right choice for you. The Miele kitchen showroom at **Arena Kitchens & Bathrooms** (3-4 Cardiff Lane, Sir John Rogerson's Quay, Dublin 2. Tel: 01-6715365) has half a dozen kitchen set-ups. Although it's possible to have a Miele kitchen for €13,000, they really start at about €18,000 and you will need to spend €40,000 for anything approaching 'the works'. Miele usually has the look of the moment (albeit diluted ever so slightly): slender glass bar handles, stainless-steel splashbacks and units that are raised from the floor as if on freestanding legs. Bulthaup (see below) started this freestanding trend, and it works, making the floor area seem larger because you see more of it. Miele is perhaps friendlier and easier to live with than austere competitors because of the way soft materials are mixed with hard: white laminate is paired with wood and solid walnut strips with matt-antiqued granite (shiny granite worktops are passé). What this kind of money buys is perfection, not to mention the satisfying swooshing of gliding drawers. If you want a good traditional kitchen, take a look at the Mark Wilkinson New England units at **Kitchen Flair** (6 Seafort Avenue, Sandymount, Dublin 4. Tel: 01-2695370); they have metal handles and geometric wood detailing. These kitchens won't date and although they can be expensive, the quality is there – they're built to last. Giving a guide price is difficult because the design is worked around your particular space but prices are from €20,000 to €50,000 on average. The price can be reduced if you cut down on extras. The New England kitchen blends well with an Aga cooker or a stainless-steel hood (better than the carved wood hood – it will keep the look a little more modern).

McNally Kitchens (46 Serpentine Avenue, Ballsbridge, Dublin 4 and M1 Business Park, Courtlough, Balbriggan, County Dublin. Tel: 01-6906000; www.mcnallyliving.ie) do very smart kitchens, including great all-black finishes. They're one of the best in the business for a high-end fitted kitchen. Their Alno range will last a lifetime and has great lighting options and clever compartments. Bulthaup kitchens (www.bulthaup.com) take themselves very seriously but with good reason: what they do is amazing. They are now available at McNally Kitchens. What you're buying is one of the most state-of-the-art kitchens available. Variations are extensive, with something new – or at least tweaked – each year. I like their suspended kitchens best. Where before this, most kitchen design was created by looking down on a floor plan and seeing how units can be configured flush to the ground, this looks to the walls instead and asks what can be hung. This means units are run in a horizontal strip along a wall, cantilevered with space above and below. It's all about engineering, as units have to hold decent weights. A Bulthaup kitchen has wonderfully thin countertops and doors and a combination of steel and oak – slightly 1950s meets space-age styling. What this means is a generally sharper appearance. Bulthaup kitchens can cost €100,000 plus – but it's possible to get a small basic one for about €30,000.

At **Lomi** (Unit 124, Baldoyle Industrial Estate, Dublin 13. Tel: 01-

8397001; www.lomi.ie) ask about the Monos range: inky-dark units and white square recessed handles with metal and white countertops. Very Milan.

Snaidero (41 Drury Street, Dublin 2. Tel: 01-6794000) is a sixty-year-old Italian kitchen company that now has a showroom in Dublin. Prices are medium to high: think €20,000 to €80,000. The location makes it easy to access and the showroom is slick, with about five kitchens on display, some traditional but most contemporary. They include all the clever additions expected of high-end kitchens, including soft-close drawers and integrated cappuccino makers, under-mounted sinks and an extensive choice of stone worktops with aluminium inlay and extractor hoods. But what's most exciting are the ranges derived from close partnerships with leading Italian designers, for example Giovanni Offredi, whose work is part of the collections of MOMA in New York and the V&A in London. In particular, see the red kitchen with continuous curving stainless-steel countertop.

If you want a old-fashioned cosy kitchen in 18th-century French or Georgian style, see the Chalon displays at **Minnie Peters** (56 Upper George's Street, Dún Laoghaire, County Dublin.

Left: An Elam kitchen, made by Italian company Tisettanta (www. tisettanta.com), in a house at the K Club furnished by **Minima**. The Elam ethos is to mix hard functionality with domestic warmth. Custom-made pieces of 'furniture' differentiate various spaces within the kitchen.

Centre: a kitchen by **McNally Kitchens**.

Right: a bespoke kitchen by interior designer **Orla Collins**.

Tel: 01-2805965). **Design House** (8 Railway Road, Dalkey, County Dublin. Tel: 01-2352222 and branches in Derry and Belfast; www.designhousedublin.com) do traditional and contemporary styles in solid woods and supply appliances; From €40,000, these kitchens are expensive but well made.

TIPS FOR THE BUDGET-CONSCIOUS

A custom-made kitchen from some of the above suppliers could cost as little as €8000 or as much as €80,000. How to save some money? Choose less expensive materials or finishes; buy good-quality cabinets and upgrade counter-tops later; spend money on the elements that are important to you and settle for the ordinary elsewhere.

Drumms (**15 Western Industrial Estate, Dublin 12. Tel: 01-4604355; www.drumms. ie) is the place to go to buy a stainless-steel sink and countertop, all in one continuous piece.** Hafele (**Kilcoole Industrial Estate, County Wicklow. Tel: 01-2873488) is where many kitchen companies get their cupboard inserts. Drawers rather than low presses are the way to go for ease of access. You can apply the same principle to your washing-up by buying a** Fisher & Paykel **dishwasher drawer.** (www.fisherpaykel.com. Tel: 1800-625174 for stockists). It's popular to have a sound system fitted in the kitchen, often with the stereo hidden inside an island unit. Niall Robinson of a company called Decibel (**Tel: 01-2967164; www.decibel.ie) will install both sound systemts and mood lighting for kitchens – dimmers, varying light for different tasks, spots over the island and so on.**

SOURCES FOR WORKTOPS

LAMINATE, CORIAN, STAINLESS STEEL, LIMESTONE, MARBLE

Artefaction (12-13 Lime Street, Dublin 2. Tel: 01-6776495): master stone masons will supply and fit a vast range of stones; **OBRE Fabrications** (Milltown Industrial Estate, Rathnew, County Wicklow. Tel: 0404-69054): for corian worktops; **Stone Developments** (Ballybrew, Enniskerry, County Wicklow. Tel: 01-2862981) supply and fit granite worktops; **DéBros Marble Works** (Ashbourne Industrial Park, Ashbourne, County Meath. Tel: 01-8353100).

SHELVING

Shelving is the workhorse of furniture. **Storage Solutions** (222 Harold's Cross,

Dublin 6w. Tel: 01-4910714, www. storagesolutions.ie) sells various combinations of clip-together chrome shelving, starting at about €120 for a four-shelf unit. Most often seen in restaurant kitchens, they are practical and attractive in an industrial sort of way. Similar systems are available from shops such as **B&Q** (nationwide**).** Plenty of open shelving is a good idea in a small kitchen. This is the approach interior designer **Karen Stafford** (karen@renovate.ie) took in the kitchen of public relations person Kate Bowe (below right): open shelving across the back wall isn't as imposing as a row of presses might be and a tall glass-fronted unit provides extra storage. **Maplewood Design** (45 Avenue Road, Dublin 8. Tel: 01-4730579) made the units.

STOOLS

For a bar or island unit, you will need stools. All the high-end kitchen companies do ranges, as do shops such as **Haus** and **Inreda**. Try **Meadows & Byrne** for painted traditional stools and **Dunnes Home** for straightforward padded stools with round seats. But **Instore** probably has the best selection – the Dome bar stool with 1950s-style black leather seat is €59, as are chrome and leather versions. A comfortable

Above: two stools from **Instore**

Below left: if possible choose drawers rather than presses for kitchen storage.

Centre: shelving from **Storage Solutions**.

Right: Kate Bowe's kitchen by **Maplewood Design**, to interior designer **Karen Stafford**'s specifications.

stool with a padded back is available for €129 – like a raised dining chair. See the suppliers' index for details of these shops.

Breakfast Tables

Looking for a chic little breakfast table? All too often furniture-makers focus on big formal affairs more fit for a state dinner than a family get-together. Meanwhile kitchen tables tend to be either big farmhouse slabs or depressing Formica holdovers. A few versions so versatile it doesn't matter what you call them – breakfast tables, kitchen tables or side tables – can be found at **Inreda** (71 Lower Camden Street, Dublin 8. Tel: 01-4760362; www.inreda.ie). They're not the cheapest you'll find but owner Frank Goodwin can order some great styles. For example, the Sandra round table by Thomas Sandell costs €1100 and is a beauty as well as being strong. They nailed the look of the legs perfectly. Another I like is the Tavolo table by Magis for €625. The base has personality. This would be equally at home in a kitchen or garden, or as an elegant side table in a living room. It has real charm and it's light enough for one person to move. Another neat version is the black Tavolo table for €495; it's slick, clean and classic. Unlike some modern pieces this could go from a country house to an apartment.

Property consultant Liz O'Kane came up with a cheaper alternative to the very large but very expensive US fridge-freezer. Behind panelled doors that match the rest of her units, she used two regular, full-size Whirlpool fridges. The doors are hinged so they open away from each other, like a cupboard. Each fridge cost €500 and she has more storage space than a US fridge would offer but she didn't have to spend €2,500.

Appliances

A good place to get an overview of almost every brand available is **Kitchen Accessories Ltd** (4078 Kingswood Road, Citywest Business Park, County Dublin. Tel: 01-4136400; www.kal.ie). They have appliances by Neff, Franke, Aga, Rayburn, InSinkErator (waste disposal) and so on. Speaking of appliances, use **Oven Clean** (Tel: 01-6615177; www.ovenclean.ie) for a thorough on-site clean of your oven.

Domini Kemp (left) shares a few kitchen must-haves: 'Whip cream, make aioli and save lumpy sauces with a Genware twelve-inch whisk (€9.30 at Sweeney O'Rourke, 34 Pearse Street, Dublin 2; Tel: 01-6777212). **A Kenwood electric hand-mixer (€24.95 at** Arnotts) **will cream eggs and sugar. A decent all-round knife is the 20cm Wusthof knife (€43 at** Sweeney O'Rourke). **Kitchen Aid does a very good food processor (€360 at** Brown Thomas). **Le Creuset casserole dishes are wonderful for roasting meat, potatoes and lasagne (from €90 at** Brown Thomas.) **Bourgeat stainless-steel pots are best for boiling spaghetti and making slow-cooked sauces and stews (approx €80 at** Sweeney & O'Rourke).

'The service that **Houseworks** give with their Siematic range is first class. Beautiful design and reliable German engineering. For a traditional style, **Chalon** (6 Main Street, Blackrock, County Dublin. Tel: 01-2835525) are expensive, but very well put together. If I had to cut my cloth, I would use a small company that can do bespoke work – a company I have worked with and has been really good at interpreting ideas is **Domino Design** in Wicklow' (01-286 6094; www. dominodesign.ie).

Bill Simpson, interior designer
e-mail: billsimpson@eircom.net

Above: Liz O'Kane with her double fridge.

Centre: Tess and Galen Bales of **www.w39. ie** hide their utilities behind panelled doors.

Left: Interior designer **Maria MacVeigh** worked on this house in Dublin choosing a moderately-priced red kitchen from **JV Kitchens** (Tel: 086-8336044). This small company is reliable and offers a good standard of workmanship. The table and chairs are from **20th-Century Furniture** at Habitat.

Bedroom

Call it new traditionalism. This headboard at Brown Thomas refers to the past but feels modern. Pure geometry, with a slightly aged paint finish, the double size pictured here costs €565. Delivery will take ten weeks. A headboard like this one is sometimes all you need – it provides low-key drama but doesn't take up floor space. To the right is a classic Bakelite lamp, designed by Robert Dudley Best in 1930 and also available at Brown Thomas for €500. The lighting section on the third floor of the Grafton Street store is the place to pick up elegant bedside lamps.

Beds

'A bedroom is both for rest and play. Key concepts for me are simplicity and lack of clutter. Soft furnishings and bedding are all part of the overall effect but restraint is an integral part of the recipe. Consider comfort, relaxation, reflection and intimacy. A bedroom should be practical with easy access to immediate needs such as storage). I used Farrow & Ball's Off White for my own bedroom walls. The windows and doors were done in their 'Pointing' shade.'

Paul Austen, interior designer
Tel: 087-2360897

Looking for a delivery man you can rely on? Beds are awkward to move and not every shop delivers. We hear one of the best in Dublin is Rick O'Shea **(Tel: 086-2616430), who comes with high recommendation from Pia Bang. He can handle large pieces and has a reputation for reliability and care with expensive items. In Cork,** Joe Murphy **(Tel: 086-8170151) is one man to contact for careful transport of furniture.**

When selecting the nightly nest of your dreams here are two things to keep in mind: (1) Is your bedmate tall? Avoid nocturnal discord by eliminating a footboard. (2) Love to sit up in bed watching TV or reading? Go for an upholstered headboard.

Low price

We Irish love a bargain. I'm desperate for the long-promised **Ikea** store to open. For example, the Malm bed at Ikea (www.ikea.com) may be basic but it's very cheap, with prices from about £75 (€110) for a single to £120 (€180) for a super king-size; the attachable bedside locker is an extra £30 (€45). These beds are particularly good for a small bedroom where you should keep things off the floor to create a

Far left top: a bedroom by interior designer **Greg Kinsella**. The bed is by Baker, an American company, which can be ordered through www.gregkinsella.ie.

Far left bottom: interior designer **Paul Austen**'s bedroom – note one soft colour palette makes for a calming space.

Below: Malm bed comes flat-pack from **Ikea**.

Left the Thurman bed, to order at **Brown Thomas**.

Top: Break up a large
headboard with padded
panels, but don't be
mean with height - let it
rise. **Fabrique** will make
something similar to this.

Centre: Bed by
Lorraine Brennan.

Bottom: platform bed
from **Duff Tisdall**.

greater feeling of space. The simple white frame looks really well against grey walls. Until Ikea opens its Irish stores in Dublin and Belfast, you'll probably have to visit the Glasgow branch, which will deliver two big trolleys of shopping to the Republic for £190 (€280). Why not club together with friends to make it worthwhile? The Monaco bed at **Argos** (branches countrywide) costs €390 for a double and has a camel-coloured panelled fabric headboard and sides. It has good proportions and says little visually: how good it looks depends on how you dress it and what you do with the rest of the room. A basic mattress is included in the price. **Muji** (5 Chatham Street, Dublin 2. Tel: 01-6794591) has a wonderful little bed with a classic frame. I like because it's unpretentious. The birch finish is slightly rough, which is lovely too. A double costs €399 and a king-size is €449. There's also a great little bedside locker to match for €299. Also try **Home Store** (Jervis Street, Dublin 1. Tel: 01-8726728) for plain timber beds and **Caseys Furniture** in Cork (65 Oliver Plunkett Street. Tel:

021-4270393) and Limerick (Raheen Roundabout, Raheen. Tel: 061-307070) for basic beds – don't expect anything too out of the ordinary; **At Home with Clerys** (Unit 2, Leopardstown Retail Park, Dublin 18. Tel: 01-2941710) is worth a look too, as is **Dunnes Home** (South Great George's Street, Dublin 2, Cornelscourt, Dublin 18, and large Dunnes Stores branches nationwide) which changes its stock regularly. See the Special section for something antique or at least antique-looking.

Mid price

The bed pictured (centre right) costs €995, a good price considering its high quality. It was designed by **Lorraine Brennan** (10 North Great George's Street, Dublin 1. Tel: 01-8735420; www.fiftyeightb.ie) for Irish manufacturer Bona Vista in County Meath (Tel: 049-8541100) and is made from dark-stained white oak with aluminium strips inserted between panels. It's strong, masculine and solid. The side tables with lights cost €200 each. Both can be seen, by appointment only at Brennan's showroom, alongside a range of her other furniture. **Duff Tisdall** (Mill Street, Dublin 8. Tel: 01-4541355 and 537 North Circular Road, Dublin 1. Tel: 01-8558070; www.duff-tisdall.ie) do a lovely plain dark-walnut bed that provides a platform for a mattress and thanks to recessed legs, looks as if it floats. At the Bray branch of **Living** (Castle Street, Bray, County Wicklow. Tel: 01-2828905; www.living.ie) you will almost always find something contemporary and reasonably priced. For a bed with a traditional look, try an **IH&G** (Irish Homes & Gardens) showroom in Dublin, Cork, Naas or Tralee (see www.ihg.ie for details). They do mahogany double sleigh beds for about €745; solid teak double Shaker styles with slatted head and floorboards from €1050 and plantation-style mahogany doubles with rattan panels for €1195. If you want a four-poster Shaker-style bed, this is where to go. At **Kilcroney Furniture** (Kilcroney, Bray, County Wicklow. Tel: 01-2829361; www.kilcroneyfurniture.ie) much of the upholstered furniture is a little old-fashioned but you will see a few

nice padded contemporary beds. You could also try: **Diamond Living** (Longmile Road and Airside Retail Park, Swords. Tel: 1850-454444; for a big solid oak bed for about €600; and **European Living** (74b Kylemore Road, Dublin 10. Tel: 01-6269005) for contemporary beds. Quality is average but you can sometimes find gems. **O'Hagan Design**, 102 Capel Street, Dublin 2. Tel: 01-872 4016) is also good for contemporary beds – particularly low platform beds. For a traditional bed try **Hilary Roche Home** (Unit A, Glencormack Business Park, Kilmacanogue, County Wicklow. Tel: 01-2723730; www.hilaryrochehome. ie) for timber cutesy beds; **Mimosa Interiors** (Cranford Centre, Stillorgan Road, Dublin 4. Tel: 01-2602443) for painted French, Gustavian and New-England styles; **Meadows & Byrne** (The Pavilion, Royal Marine Road, Dún Laoghaire, County Dublin. Tel: 01-2804554), for padded leather beds; **Fired Earth** (20 Lower George's Street, Dún Laoghaire, County Dublin. Tel: 01-6636160; www.firedearth.com) for Elizabethan/Tudor style beds, if you like that kind of thing; **Flanagans Of Buncrana** (Deerpark Road, Mount Merrion. Tel: 01-2880218) sometimes have the odd interesting thing in an antique look. For sleigh beds and other traditional styles, try the **Linenmill** (The Demesne, Westport, County Mayo. Tel: 098-29500; www.linenmillshop. com). **Habitat** (6-10 Suffolk Street, Dublin 2. Tel: 01-6771433; Fairgreen Road, Galway. Tel: 091-569980; and 41 Arthur Street, Belfast BT1 4GB. Tel: 028-90249522) is good for modern four-poster beds, such as the Hana bed (dark wood, very slender four-poster frame) which costs €860. Potter **Nicholas Mosse** (Bennetsbridge, County Kilkenny. Tel: 056-7727505) has branched into furniture and makes a four-poster wood bed to order.

High end

If money is no object and you want something contemporary but subtly out of the ordinary you should consider the **Bedroom Studio** (26 Castle Street, Dalkey, County Dublin. Tel: 01-2352815; www.bedroomstudio.ie). Father and son owners Martin and

Paul Buckley have a long association with the making and selling of beds: Martin's grandfather started a bed-making business in 1926. About a dozen beds are on view in the shop, but many more can be ordered. Most are from Italian, French or Spanish companies, and there are other bedroom bits and pieces. Beds by Flou will appeal to those who like something 'unobtrusive'. There are also a few traditional styles, and dramatic art-deco-inspired beds in ebony. **Brown Thomas**'s (Grafton Street, Dublin 2. Tel: 01-6056666) dramatic Thurman bed (to order) has a very high button back and costs from €5600, depending on fabric. It has a light-hearted appeal. Ask to see the Capellini beds catalogue at **Haus** (Crow Street and Pudding Row, Temple Bar, Dublin. Tel: 01-6795155; www.haus.ie). Discreet lines make these beds very soft visually and prices start at about €3000. They are usually finished in fabrics that won't compete with anything else in a room. **Design Flow** (Unit 1B, Distillery Court, 537 North Circular Road, Dublin 7. Tel: 01-8349712; www.designflow.ie) deals

Top: bed from **Living**.

Bottom: bed from the **Bedroom Studio**.

Top left: Nikki Bonass reclines againt a custom headboard by **Merrion Square Interior**s.

Top right: a romantic carved bed from **Minnie Peters**.

Bottom right: a dressing table, chair and mirror from the third floor of **Brown Thomas.**

Bottom left: a Knowles & Christou mirrored dressing table available from Philippa Buckley (**www.studio44.ie**).

mostly with the trade and doesn't have a shop as such, but interior-designer owner Robert Trench will place orders for a great bed by ALF Group: it has clean lines, a slightly curved headboard and a simple Japanese feel. The mattress sits on to the base rather than into it and a double costs €1452. Art deco dealer Niall Mullen (**Niall Mullen Antiques**, 105 Francis St, Dublin 8. Tel: 01-4538948) often has bed frames and bedroom sets that can run up to seven pieces (and five-digit prices). **Greg Kinsella Interiors** (Parnell Road, Bray, County Wicklow. Tel: 01-2868017; www.gregkinsella.com) are agents for furniture by Baker, an American company that does polished beds, reminiscent of 1930s Hollywood (think €8000). See picture on p.72. The **French Warehouse** (www.french-warehouse.com. Tel: 028-44839360) is a company in County Down that specialise in importing antique beds from France – 19th-century mahogany beds, headboards and four-poster beds with gilt details. Romantic four-poster beds can also be found at **Dream Beds** (65 Francis Street, Dublin 8. Tel:

01-4546626) from a simple walnut version at €3000 to a Regency antique bed at €9000. This is the place to go if you want something that looks like an antique but in a regular size. For a fabric- or leather-padded bed with high back **Orior** (12 Greenbank Industrial Estate, Newry, County Down. Tel: 028-30262620; ww.oriorbydesign.com) make the Aspen bed from €3500. Orior have a showroom but will accept orders only through an interior designer or **Peter Johnson** (6 Lombard Street, Dublin 8. Tel: 01-453088) and **Minnie Peters** (56–7 Upper George's Street, Dún Laoghaire, County Dublin. Tel: 01-2805965). Contact these shops to see what's available and ask about prices.

New wrought-iron headboards can be bought from €195 at Yesterday Once More (**3 Carysfort Avenue, Blackrock, County Dublin. Tel: 01-2108410; www. yesterdayoncemore.ie**). Murphy & Quinlan **in Douglas Street, Cork (Tel: 021-4321021) sell restored wrought-iron beds from €400.**

FABRIC HEADBOARDS

A custom-made headboard can do a lot for an ordinary bed. **Fabrique Interiors** (Tel: 01-8241716) in Dunshaughlin, County Meath, sell good fabrics and can make a headboard to exact measurements by a craftsman who works at nothing else. Almost any shape is possible – curves or geometric designs – and delivery is generally about a week. Another good headboard-maker is **Ray Shannon Headboards** (52 Cork Street, Dublin 8. Tel: 01-4532889).

BEDSIDE LOCKERS AND DRESSING TABLES

All the shops listed above sell night stands, bedside lockers and dressing tables. Lack of space means that I can show you only my current favourites. The bedside locker I like most is available through **Peter Johnson Interiors.** It's functional, with little storage 'boxes', but interesting, and reminds me of a Mondrian painting. It costs €595.

The Mimi dressing table (see previous page) is French 1940s

meets Hollywood glam – how's that for a combo? It's available through **www.studio44.ie** and costs €3850. There are two drawers and a fold-up vanity mirror. The legs are oak (it is also available in black) and there's a matching stool. Instead of a mirror, you can order etched or printed glass.

FOOTSTOOLS

A footstool can add zing to a bedroom, at the bottom of a bed or under a window. The **Collection** (Unit 4, St Helen's Court, Lower George's Street, Dún Laoghaire, County Dublin. Tel: 01-2147700; www.the-collection. ie) do long suede ones for €700 (ask about The Warhol range) and **KA International** (Main Street, Blackrock, County Dublin. Tel: 01-2782033 and Jervis Shopping Centre, Dublin 1. Tel: 01-8781052; branches also in Cork, Galway and Enniskerry; see www. kainternational.ie for details) have a multitude of versions at mid-price points.

MATTRESSES

A significant portion of life is spent sleeping so don't end up on a bed of nails. It might sound obvious but before you buy a mattress, lie on it. Don't be guided by price. You might not find the dearest the most comfortable. **Arnotts** (Henry Street, Dublin 1. Tel: 01-8050400), for example, has thirty-five mattresses on show, all of good quality but varying prices. Remember that mattresses that are pocket sprung (individual coils) are generally better than coil sprung (one continuous coil) because they adapt to the body's shape more easily. But no-spring, slow-release beds are the future. Tentur's mattress at Arnotts, for example, takes your body shape and then slowly returns to its original shape when you get up. It's longer-lasting too, which explains the high price: €3630 (with divan).

Ask if the Irish Chiropractic Association approves a mattress. One that has this approval is the King Coil Posture Support mattress, good for those who like a firm bed. The coil springs inside are tighter than normal and hidden inside the bed are thin metal strips that provide further back

support. A 4'6" divan costs €970.

Futons aren't for everyone, but a good
one should give your spine both comfort
and support. At **Living Quarters** (Bank
House, Cornmarket, Dublin 8. Tel: 01-
6717998) Akita's futon is one of the best.
It comes flat-packed and costs €299.

Some of the best mattresses I've come
across are at **Classic Furniture**. The
Carrickmines, County Dublin, branch
(Tel: 01-2076566) has an excellent
mattress section, including plenty of latex
options. A latex bed will stop dust from
festering.

BEDLINEN

A beautiful bed is life-enhancing and
can help make you wake up feeling
good, maybe even happy. Make sure
you've got a decent mattress and two
square pillows to sit behind regular ones.
Dressing a bed is like dressing yourself:
use things that feel good against the skin:
layer blankets, duvets and textures. Peel
back each blanket or throw so you see
a little of each. My favourite bedlinen
shop is **Bottom Drawer** at Brown Thomas
in Dublin and Cork. Nancy Duffin and
three of her children – Arlene, Lisa and

Ray – have been selling the best bedlinen and bathroom goods from established names such as Frette and fashion brands such as Missoni for almost twenty years. In Bottom Drawer you will find the extraordinary (sable throws for €3500) and the inexpensive (beautiful linen tea towels for €10).

Antique linen has two advantages: it can be cheaper to buy and has been softened with age. Two antique linen sheets sewn together creates the ultimate luxury duvet cover. Find old linens at the antique fairs held at the Tara Towers Hotel, in Booterstown, County Dublin once a month. Keep an eye on the Saturday antiques pages of *The Irish Times* **for details.** Jenny Vander **(50 Drury Street, Dublin 2. Tel: 01-6770406) has white damask duvet covers from the 1950s; prices start at about €60.**

It's not good if the only time you write is when you sign cheques. So indulge in stationery. Customise cards and scribble notes from your bed. Friends will be delighted. Lavery Personalised Stationery **(01-4649829; www.lavery.ie) does a box of 100 letterheads, 50 cards and 100 matching envelopes for €158.**

Tep: Amadio Mirage
wardrobe by Interni,
available from
Classic Furniture.

Centre and bottom: go
to **McNally Living** for
quality mid- to high-
end contemporary
wardrobes, standard
and walk-in options.

WARDROBES

LOW PRICE

The **Panelling Centre** (109 Longmile
Rd, Walkinstown, Dublin 12. Tel:
01-4564899 and Sallynoggin Road.
Tel: 01-2849988) is the best place to
get an inexpensive built-in wardrobe
that's perfectly plain but looks good.
€600 will go a long way. Small, two-
door, freestanding wardrobes can be
found in most furniture shops but,
generally, built-ins are better. **Habitat**
do freestanding wardrobes that are
totally plain, usually in black-stained
oak with press and release doors. Just
don't try to assemble one yourself – life
is too short! Also at Habitat, see white
lacquer bedroom storage units of all
kinds: cabinets, tallboys and chests.

MID PRICE

Classic Furniture does slick-looking
wardrobes with great inserts and prices
that start from €1200. Go there for an
elegant modern wardrobe in a high-
gloss lacquered finish. This is actually a
great one-stop place for the bedroom:
they also do chests with an ebony-like

veneer (see back cover pictures, from
€750) and red laminates (about €1500)
– all very Milanese. **Houseworks** (11-
15 Upper Erne Street, Dublin 2. Tel:
01-6769511; www.houseworks.ie)
also do discreet built-in wardrobes.
Keatings Fitted Furniture (Ballyhooley
Road, Ballyvolvane, Cork. Tel: 021-
4506500; www.keatingfurniture.com)
supply Hülsta wardrobes: big glossy
sliding panel doors in great colours,
with aluminium and glass. Everything
is straightforward enough – but often
that's just fine. Prices start at about
€1000. **Kelco Designs** (Unit 18,
Churchtown Business Park, Beaumount
Avenue, Churchtown, Dublin 14.
Tel: 01-2965500; www.kelcodesigns.
com) are best at making conventional
and walk-in wardrobes in a traditional
classic style: imagine a room panelled,
painted and with compartments for
everything!

HIGH END

If you're taking about really good
construction, look at the Veneran range
at **Minima** (8 Herbert Place, Dublin
2. Tel: 01-6627894; www.minima.ie)

which starts at about €5700. It does what it has to do but looks fantastic from the outside. It has wing doors (so they fold open flat) and a glossy lacquer finish. The back of the piece is finished, so it can stand away from a wall, plus it's freestanding so you can take it away if you move – important when furniture is this expensive.

At Minima you can also also order wardrobes by Tisettanta (www. tisettanta.com), one of the best modern wardrobe-makers. **McNally Living** (46 Serpentine Avenue, Ballsbridge, Dublin 4 and M1 Business Park, Courtlough, Balbriggan, County Dublin. Tel: 01-6906000; www.mcnallyliving.ie) has now branched into wardrobes: think high quality, perfect finishes and an elegant look. You'll need to spend at least €3000. See the storage section in Around the House for ideas about chests of drawers.

Bathroom

Habitat has a small, perennial range of mid-price free-standing sinks. This console model has a sexy black glass counter with an ever-popular ceramic bowl sink. It costs €550 and would be suitable for an unconventional bathroom, perhaps one in a period house, as it doesn't interfere too much with the architecture – use it in a room you don't want to feel like a bathroom. Habitat usually does a variation of this with a wood storage unit beneath the sink.

'It's important in a small bathroom to keep as much as possible off the floor (i.e. have the sink and toilet wall-mounted), so you can see all corners of the room – it makes the space seem larger. Have the walls and floor clad in the same material: don't break up a small space further by using too many materials. In a small bathroom there should be just one main feature, usually the sink.'

Deirdre Danaher, interior designer
Tel: 01-2880380

Here are my ten favourite bathroom shops, in absolutely no particular order. Go to them for a complete service or just for fittings.

1. **BTW** (www.btw.ie) stands for bathrooms, tiles and wood floors and is a comprehensive showroom in what was once the Tile Savers premises on Dublin's North Wall Quay. Other branches are located in Sandyford, Tallaght, Naas, Newbridge, Mullingar, Dundalk,

Bray, Wexford, Kilkenny, Clonmel and Castelbar. It's a one-stop shop: the selection of sanitaryware is broad with prices starting low and rising high-ish for showstopper pieces. Tiling and flooring options are displayed in large panels. At the moment, it seems the larger the tile, the quicker it sells. Fashion stylist Niamh O'Rourke bought tiles here when renovating her bathroom and recommends tiler **Ciara Jordan** (087-6969285): 'She did a perfect job fast.'

2. Interior designer Deirdre Whelan used a sink from **Elegant John** (70 North Wall Quay, Dublin 1. Tel: 01-8658010; www.elegantjohn.ie) in her Rathmines home (see opposite page, top). It's called Scola and is made by Duravit. She put it on a wood pedestal to create storage underneath, but also because it's lovely to have a freestanding sink in front of a window. The wall to the left is mirrored. Elegant John is synonymous with high-end quality and prices but you'll find some reasonable stuff here too, including a good range of suspended 'shelf'-like sinks (i.e. no pedestal). This shop is very good for problem-solving fittings. Period houses, for example, often throw up the possibility of transforming a small bedroom into a bathroom. The room property consultant Liz O'Kane chose to turn into a family bathroom (see opposite page, bottom) was particularly narrow and it was hard to fit in all the necessary sanitaryware. A shower-over-bath usually means installing the shower head at the top of the bath but with the window at one end of the room and the door at the other there wasn't enough wall space. The solution was a Huppe shower enclosure from Elegant John that folds flat against the bath wall. It is fitted in the middle of the wall and the screen folds out to create an enclosure and then folds back flat. Prices start at €1400.

Top: interior designer Deirdre Whelan's bathroom with sink from **Elegant John**. Note the recessed strip lighting.

Bottom: shower with flat-folding screen by **Elegant John**.

3. **Ideal Bathrooms** (Lower Ballymount Road, Walkinstown, Dublin 12. Tel: 01-4609911; www.idealbathrooms.com) are strong on combined basin and storage units. For example, a Villeroy & Boch double basin set in a long panel of dark-stained wood with storage beneath can cost about €2000. Baths tend to come in three lengths: 1600mm, 1800mm or 1900mm. Buy as long a bath as your room will allow. If you have an awkward space, Ideal Bathrooms has baths that are thinner at one end. Prices start at €750. Think about a jacuzzi bath – the extra expense is worthwhile and this shop has versions that aren't flashbacks to 1983.

4. Sean Eacrett, a one-time antiques dealer on Francis Street, now owns **Ashgrove Interiors** (Ballybrittas, County Laois. Tel: 057-8626290.) It's a large purpose-built complex that combines the sale of antiques with contemporary furniture and also some rather up-to-the-minute bathroom fittings: in particular look at those by Lineabeta. They're cool but timeless – see their square sinks.

5. **The Victorian Salvage & Joinery Company** (South Glouchester Street, Dublin 2. Tel: 01-6727000) is the place to go to find a cast-iron bath or an antique-looking shower fitting. You can also find old-fashioned taps and quarry tiles for the floor. The company makes panelled surrounds for baths, with mirror insets and storage to the sides.

6. Go to **Fired Earth** (31 Lower Ormond Quay, Dublin 1. Tel: 01-8735362 and 20 Lower George's St, Dún Laoghaire, County Dublin. Tel: 01-6636160) for traditional sanitaryware and tiles. Imagine chunky rectangular white porcelain sinks and baths. For example, the 'Greenwich' basin and chrome stand costs about €900 and is wonderfully 1940s-ish. Its neat size makes it suitable for a small

bathroom. The Versailles cast-iron bath costs €1800 and a classic bath mixer is €1100. The Dún Laoghaire showroom also has an extensive selection of bathroom tiles, including rectangular ones fashioned after 'subway' tiles for €45 per square metre.

7. The word 'texture' is a common one in interiors magazines nowadays, and concrete is a textural as it gets. When used properly it doesn't look brutal or austere but rather luxurious. **Antica** (The Stone Gallery, Earlscourt Industrial Estate, Beaumount Avenue, Churchtown, Dublin 14. Tel: 01-2960136; www.antica.ie),

the stone specialist company, has recently started to sell rectangular polished cement sinks and shower trays in grey, white or red tints, at prices that are not low but not unattainable either, starting at about €1250. Antica, as you probably already know, is the place to go for very fine stones, which are impressive and expensive. It's all about subtleties of the colour and the quarries they are sourced from. Their travertine and limestone baths start at about €15,000 and are carved from a solid piece of stone. Because stone is several inches thick, water will stay hot longer, but the real reason people buy these baths is for their spare, elegant

Left: a bath from **Fired Earth**.

Centre: a sink, also from **Fired Earth**.

Right: a wet-room-style shower with mosaics from **Mosaic Assemblers**.

look. But consider the weight: your bathroom floor had better be able to take it. Ask your builder or architect. Another place for stone is **Rocca Stone and Marble** (Unit 2, Site 21, Canal Walk, Park West, Dublin 12. Tel: 01-6205607; www.roccastone.com). They don't have quite the same quality as Antica but are good if you want the look. By the way, **Alan Ward** (087-6308078) has been mentioned by a number of interior designers as a supplier who deals in the best stones but at prices that are not beyond most people's reach. He will also fit the stone.

8. Even with the sterling exchange, the **Yard** (Montgomery Road, Belfast. Tel: 028-90405600; www.theyard.co.uk) is worth a visit if you want something really special. A little off the beaten track at the end of a lane in an industrial park, it's renowned for stocking the best bathroom fittings in the North, from the spectacular (a glass bath for £21,000) to the affordable (from £200). For example, in textile designer Liz Nilsson's bathroom, it was hard to accommodate the necessary sanitaryware because a doorway dominated one wall and a window filled the other. So a sink from the Yard was placed under the window, with a mirror rising in front of the opening.

9. Over the past twenty years Catherine Treacy has created an impressive shop at **Versatile Bathrooms (**Beechmount Industrial Estate, Navan, County Meath. Tel: Tel: 046-9029444 www.versatile.ie). It appeals to a cross-section of customers, but what makes the shop stand out is service – you can trust that things will go smoothly. It has leading design and quality brands and offers every kind of style, including very minimal fittings. Here you will find extra-deep baths costing from €600 to €1000. Compact 1930s sinks and toilets are perfect for small en-suites: see the Duravit range from €1200. The shop also has plenty

Clockwise from top left: a bathroom scene by **Antica**, stone specialists. Note the shallow rectangular glass sink; textile designer Liz Nilsson's sink from the **Yard** in Belfast; a high-tech shower, part of the range of fittings available at **Antica**; a bath by **Driftwood** (23 Glendale Drive, Bray, County Wicklow. www.driftwood.ie). This company makes rectangular and oval solid wood baths with a Bali-esque vibe. Prices start at about €2000 depending on the wood chosen. For example, the American black walnut 'ofuro' (Japanese-style) bath measures 1000 x 600 x 715 mm and costs €2900.

Top: a bath from the **Yard** in Belfast – a mere £21,000.

Centre: a bathroom designed by Simon O'Driscoll using mirror to make the narrow space seem larger. The walls and floor are covered in tiny round tiles from **Mosaic Assemblers**. There's nothing superfluous, such as skirting boards – this gives the room a streamlined look and makes it easier to clean. The sink and toilet hang from the wall, which also aids cleaning and makes the room seem larger. The chair is by Gio Ponti.

Bottom: Ceramic soap dish from **Debenhams**. Try their Homewares department for bathroom accessories.

of variations of the thing of the moment: square shallow glass sinks.

10. **Surface** in Dún Laoghaire (Surface Ceramics, 69 Upper George's Street, Dún Laoghaire, County Dublin. Tel: 01-6638991) is perhaps better known for tiles but also has a bathroom showroom at a separate premises nearby (Surface Bathrooms, Ashgrove Industrial Estate, Kill Avenue, Dún Laoghaire, County Dublin. Tel: 01-6637803; www.surface.ie.) The best-known brand they carry is Alessi but you will also see bathroom sets with innovative, modern fittings. These bathrooms are streamlined and non-fuss but still groovy. At Surface you'll get expertise and good style advice. They also do great floor tiles – choose a surface that's slip-resistant even when wet yet easy to clean. There are beautiful stones at Surface too. Look at the Ardesia range – a very natural textured porcelain tile for both floors and walls with an organic contemporary

look. I like the narrow vertical-strip mosaic tiles. Also see porcelain, mosaic, glass and Victorian tiles.

Be optimistic and buy a double-ended bath (for potential sharing) with taps at the side rather than one end.

ALSO TRY

Waterloo Bathrooms in Dún Laoghaire (Tel: 01-2842100); **Davies Bathrooms** in Raheny and Wicklow (Tel: 01-8511700); **H$_2$0 Pumps** in Kilternan, County Dublin (specialists in tap ware and showers. Tel: 01-2822025); **Tubs & Tiles** (in the company's branches countrywide, you'll find a huge range of straightforward fittings; www.tubstiles.ie); **City Building Supplies** (4 Curzon Street, Dublin 8. Tel: 01-4542633) for Duravit, Roca, Shires and Grohe; **Heritage Bathrooms** (Block 5, Link Business Park, Kilcullen, County Kildare. Tel: 045-480899); **Bathrooms 2000** (Southbank Industrial Estate, Marsh Road, Drogheda, County Louth. Tel: 041-9845455; www.bathrooms2000.com): great for jacuzzi baths.

All the shops above sell tiles but also look at **VitrA Ireland** (North Ring Business Park, Santry and South Quay, Arklow, 01-8165588); **Stone & Tile Affair** (Tramore Road, Cork. Tel: 021-4311248); **Kilkenny Tile Store** (7 Irishtown, Kilkenny. Tel: 056-7763099). **Regan Tile Design** (2 Corrig Avenue, Dún Laoghaire, County Dublin. Tel: 01-2800921) is good for grey slate tiles; **Porcelanosa** (Unit 180, Oak Road, Western Industrial Estate, Dublin 12. Tel: 01-4197988; www.porcelanosa.com) is a Spanish tile manufacturer that does large metallic-look tiles – they are porcelain with an oxidised steel finish; **Plaza Ceramics** (Santry Hall Industrial Estate, Santry, Dublin 9. Tel: 01-8429744; www.plazatiles.com) have an Indian Slate range of porcelain tiles with a rustic stone look – colours are black, copper and silver.

Always have lights with a dimmer switch in a bathroom: at night or if you're sick it's better not to have a full glare.

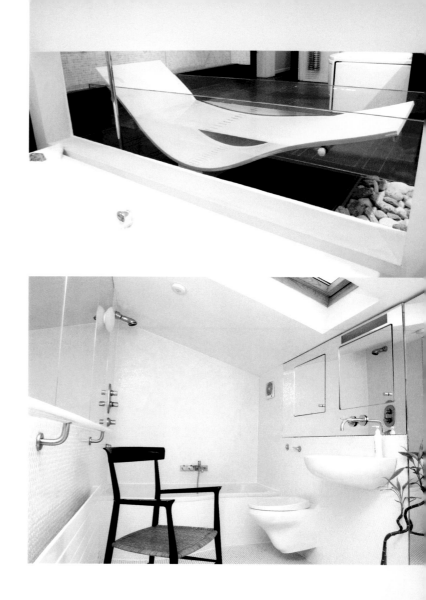

Home Store & More in Belgard Road, Dublin 24. (Tel: 01-4610430) is good for low-cost bathroom accessories, such as mirrored bathroom cabinets for €50.

For small areas that need to be tiled, **Mosaic Assemblers** (Unit 14, The Courtyard, Fonthill Industrial Estate, Dublin 22. Tel: 01-6267669) sells end-of-line mosaics from €25 a square metre and mixed boxes of mosaic for €40.

The **Glass Centre** (Goldenbridge Industrial Estate, Inchicore, Dublin 8. Tel: 01-4541711) sometimes has odd pieces of mirror that they sell off very cheaply – with some luck they'll have the size you need.

There's an odds-and-ends feel to the **Arnotts Bargain Shop** (Middle Abbey Street, Dublin 1). You've got to pick through brown fleece blankets to find the good stuff that's filtered down from the main shop: for example, cheap sisal floor rugs, goose-down duvets reduced to half price, good quality bath sheets for about a tenner and accessories for the bathroom.

Most bathroom shops will fit sanitaryware themselves or recommend a good plumber. If not, try **Alliance Property Maintenance** (Unit Q6, Greenogue Business Park, Rathcoole, County Dublin. Tel: 01-4013970), a company doing complete renovations and building work as well as plumbing, tiling, electrics and general carpentry. They may charge a little more than others but they're hassle-free.

Smell good. Your bathroom should be in a constant cloud of Orange Blossom fragrance from L'Occitane **(Wicklow St, Dublin 2. Tel: 01-6797223, www.loccitane. com). Extracted from the marmalade tree, it is the most delicious scent. L'Occitane does a room spray for €19.95 (keep some in the bathroom) and an eau de toilette for €39.95 (put this in the hall for a quick squirt on your way out). There's also a candle, incense and soap.**

A **wet room** is a fully waterproofed bathroom without enclosures. The walls of the bathroom form the boundaries of the shower. That means no shower tray and an optional glass panel to partly screen the shower. Water is allowed to fall across the floor and steam fills the space, giving a steam-room feel to your shower. The most important thing to get right is the details: most importantly, water must flow towards a drain. If this is in the middle of the room, you will need to have the sides of the room built up above the level of the drain. Creating a leak-proof room is complex too: the structure of the room must be very stable (ground floor is better than first) and waterproofed with a layer of fibreglass or lead. A wet room is ideal for a small bathroom where enclosing the shower in a separate cubicle would encroach on the space but a small wet room is not the best place for storage. In larger wet rooms, storage can be fitted well away from the shower. Apart from tiling, various types of stone are popular choices for wet-room cladding but even wood can be used if sealed.

Top: a bathroom by interior designer **Karen Stafford**, clad in travertine marble from **Rocca Marble & Stone**.

Bottom: Ceramic basin by Quibic Crafts (www. quibiccrafts.com). The range is inspired by African art with prices from €700. See them at **Davies Bathrooms** (Tel: 01-8511700).

BATHROOM

The wet room in Jason Lawless's house (pictured on page 99) provides a few good examples of what must be done if you want this kind of bathroom. Because his shower space is quite open, the concrete floor is sloped so water flows to the drain underneath the showerhead.

The tiles Jason used non-slip grey porcelain from **Lomac Tiles** (72 North Wall Quay Dublin 1. Tel: 01 8551588) are quite large and proved tricky to lay on a sloped floor – with hindsight, he says, small tiles such as mosaic would have been easier. But thanks to a good tiler (**Terry Lawton**. Tel: 087-2848870) they did work.

Under-floor heating is also a must: water splashes beyond the toughened glass panels but when the floor is warm it dries almost instantly. Then, because the room is all one tiled space, the underfloor heating runs right into the shower so your feet are warm beneath the water. The power shower is by Grohe at **Davies Bathrooms** (150 Harmonstown Road, Raheny, Dublin 5. Tel: (01-8511700) and has body jets and other features. The fittings are concealed behind the wall to keep a clean look.

Jason used plumber **Niall O'Dwyer** (Tel: 086-8237435) for this work.) The sink counter top is Portuguese marble from **Marble & Granite Supplies.** (Coolock Industrial Estate Dublin 17. Tel: 01-8671077). The total cost from scratch of everything you see here – fittings, tiles, labour and so on – was about €8000.

OTHER TIPS

Working through architects or interior designers, **Tru Curve** (Grand Canal Business Centre, Dublin 8. Tel: 01-4730710) will supply and fit shower screens to practically any size – curved glass is a speciality.

Renu Bath (78 Walkinstown Road, Dublin 12. Tel: 01-4500433) restores and resurfaces old baths.

Flair International are the Irish manufacturers of glass shower enclosures and bath screens. See www.flairshowers.com for stockists or to request a brochure.

FitzMawn Interiors & Tiles (Deansgrange Business Park, Kill

Avenue, Blackrock, County Dublin. Tel: 01-2898822; www.fitzmawninteriors. ie) is run by interior designer Trish Fitzpatrick. The showroom offers a lot of alternative stones, marbles, porcelains you won't find elsewhere, all nicely displayed. Imagine unusual colours and textures but in particular, I like their very large tiles, almost like wall panels. The shop is also good for traditional style fittings, such as a 'slipper'-shape claw-foot baths (higher at one end than the other).

Glasshammer Design (Rhode, County Offaly. Tel: 046-9739290; www.glasshammer.ie) specialise in glass and mosaic. They make furniture but will also do things such as create layers of laminate glass to frame a shower. Glass can be etched and sandblasted – see the website for a better idea. This won't be to everyone's taste but they have great skills. Go to them with a very clear idea about what you want or bring an interior designer. They also make glass wall panels, often with melded copper strips, that could be used to divide an open bedroom and bathroom space.

Red or black bathroom suites are fashionable but beware the avocado syndrome – colour can seem like a good idea but you'll grow tired of it fast. White really is the only option.

Left: Jason Lawless's wet-room bathroom.

Right: **VitrA Ireland** retro design.

BATHROOM

99

KIDS' ROOM

INSTORE IS AN IRISH-OWNED CHAIN OF FURNITURE SHOPS WITH BRANCHES IN LIMERICK, GALWAY, SLIGO AND WATERFORD. PRICES ARE MODERATE AND FOR CHILDREN'S ROOMS, THEY ALWAYS HAVE A GOOD RANGE OF CUTE BEDS. PICTURED RIGHT, FOR EXAMPLE, IS A CURVED METAL BED WITH ALABASTER FINISH WHICH COSTS €169. THERE ARE ALSO SWEET LITTLE NIGHTSTANDS, PRACTICAL WARDROBES AND DEEP CHESTS OF DRAWERS AND WHAT'S BEST ABOUT THEIR KIDS' FURNITURE IS THAT IT'S ALL REASONABLY ROBUST.

Furniture for children's bedrooms
and playrooms is often either horribly
twee, ridiculously dayglo or boringly
functional. **Amelia Aran** (71 York Road,
Dún Laoghaire, County Dublin. Tel:
01-2805877; www.ameliaaran.com),
a Spanish company, makes furniture
that is sweet but simple and comes in
soft colours that are more compatible
with homes that are decorated in
contemporary style. This shop, the only
branch outside Spain, was opened by
Áine McCarthy. What sells best are
bunk beds and tumble beds (sofas with
pull-out beds beneath), from €1215.
One of the cutest beds for boys has
blue ships sailing across its headboard.
Other lovely things include chests of
drawers (€1040), bookcases (€626) and
tables (€432) which can all be ordered

in various lacquered finishes.

Peoba (River Court, River Lane, Dundalk, County Louth. Tel: 042-9354222) specialises in furniture and bedlinen for children's rooms. Sinéad O'Callaghan, who owns the shop, has gathered together furniture such as lockers, drawers and wardrobes that are part-Swedish and part-English in style. Beds and cradles use undyed fabrics and anti-allergenic mattresses. There are accessories such as the colourful boxes pictured opposite, and the shop also offers an interior design service for children's playrooms and bedrooms.

Limari (7 Donnybrook Mall, Dublin 4. Tel: 01-2602420; www.limari.ie) sells colourful cots, beds, wardrobes, desks, side lockers and dressing tables.

Left: a child's bed from **Limari**, Donnybrook, Dublin.

Right: a child's bed from **McNally Living**.

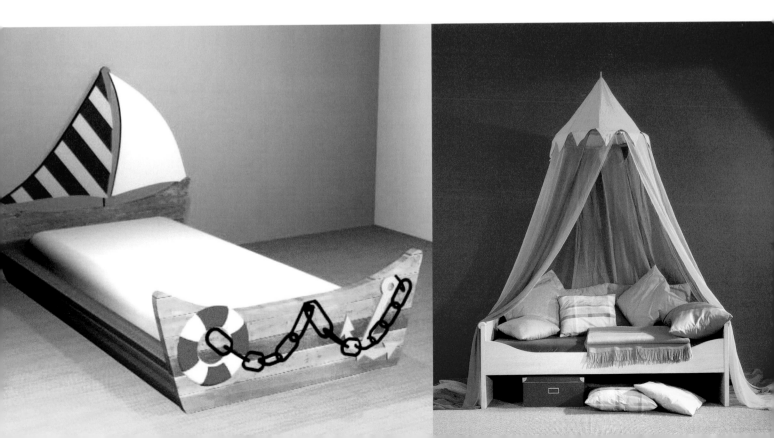

Left: hangers from
Triple Star.

Centre: bunk beds from
Classic Furniture.

Right: desk by
Clever Clogs.

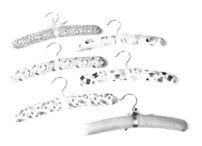

There are also very clever storage units perfect for play areas. Designed to last, most things are made from oak. Customers can visit Limari with the dimensions of their child's room and have a 3-D layout created, making it possible to see how items will actually look before making any purchase. Apart from furniture, Limari stocks the most beautiful hand-embroidered bedlinen and curtains. Customers can also have fabrics designed to their particular tastes to match themes they may already have in their homes. Very cute mini-sofas and chairs are available in nine different shades of leather.

The padded hangers above are from **Triple Star**, the children's clothing and accessories company set up a few years ago by Paula Flynn (former vice-president of Baby Gap) and Sheila Rasmussen (interior and textile designer). As with everything the pair produce, inspiration for the prints used came from playful vintage graphics from the 1930s, 1940s and 1950s. They have a nice handcrafted look and cost €19.95 for three, from Jane Carroll (details below, or www.triplestar.com)

Clever Clogs import kids' furniture from the Netherlands and Denmark, in particular Danish cradle company Leanderform and Dutch blanket specialist Lodger. The Leander cradle is suspended from a ceiling hook or tripod stand and provides smooth and soothing rocking movements. These motions closely replicate the natural movements of a baby in the womb. The optional drape gently diffuses light into the cradle, heightening the soothing and calming effect. The mattress is asthma- and allergy-friendly and all fabrics used in the cradle are undyed and can be washed. The Leander cradle comes recommended by the Danish Premature Babies Association and is proven to aid sleep in babies suffering from colic or stress. Suitable from birth through to five-six months. Prices start at €190. Available at **Nelo Maternity** (39 Clarendon St, Dublin 2. Tel: 01-6791336 and **Little People** (Ballyogan Road, Dublin 18. Tel: 01-2999796); for other stockists countrywide see www. cleverclogs.ie).

One of F. Scott Fitzgerald's heroines once lamented: 'I never noticed the stars before, I always thought of them as great big diamonds that belonged to someone.' A few stars – and

snowflakes, too – definitely worth noticing are those available from **Childhood Interiors** (www.childhoodinteriors.co.uk), a UK-based web company that will deliver to Ireland. The large graphic wall decorations can be bought as a pack of three or more, costing from €73 per set, and can be ordered in white, black or a mirrored finish. Use in a random pattern on a wall.

Jane Carroll (62a Carysfort Avenue, Blackrock, County Dublin. Tel: 01-2783925) is a tiny shop selling small painted pieces of furniture such as wood chairs and wall clocks. She also has the best duvets and bedlinen for toddlers' beds. Everything has a home-made feel, in the best sense. Great for gifts, too.

Left: Jane Carroll in her Blackrock shop.

Right: a child's bed from **Minnie Peters**.

HOME OFFICE

At fashion stylist Niamh O'Rourke's home office, an archimoon desk lamp by philip starck has a shade made from pleated fabric. it costs €315 at Haus and delivery usually takes about four weeks. You'll find small-scale desks similar to Niamh's at Habitat.

Don't be afraid to think outside the box – browse junk shops for items that can be repurposed as storage containers. Instead of standard 'in-and-out' boxes, try a few whimsical canvas bins from **Next** (67 Grafton St Dublin 2. Tel: 01-6793300 and branches countrywide) or a pair of brightly-coloured or silver serving trays from **Brown Thomas** (Grafton Street, Dublin 2. Tel: 01-6056666). Clear the clutter and eliminate the distractions. Things you use every day belong where you can see them – on the desk. Less frequently used items can be stored in desk drawers, cabinets or storage containers. **Muji** (5 Chatham Street, Dublin 2. Tel: 01-6794591) is wonderful for all office-y bits and pieces.

At home it's better to have a great-looking desk and comfortable chair than an ugly office-style work station.

DESKS, CHAIRS AND LIGHTS

An Irish company called **Nest** (Unit 4, Midleton Enterprise Centre, Knockgriffin, Midleton, County Cork. Tel: 021-4630659; www.nest-design. com), operated by designers Annabel and Neil McCarthy, is known for the high quality of its joinery and finish. The desk pictured on the opposite page is called the Twist and is made from pear wood with a high-gloss Japanese lacquer finish. It is made to order and costs approximately €1960.

The new Bordonabe range of office furniture by renowned Spanish designer Francesc Rife is available at **Bob Bushell** (Sir John Rogerson's Quay, Dublin 2. Tel: 01-6710044; www. bobbushell.com). This shop is one of the best for home office furniture. For example, the Movie Star desk by Gallotti & Radice costs €895 and is made from specially strengthened glass. Glass storage units and shelving are also available. This desk sits neatly into a corner and because it's transparent, doesn't appear to take up a lot of space.

Inside Interiors (3 Heather Rd, Sandyford Industrial Estate, Dublin 18. Tel: 01-2943869) do a lot of contract furniture, working with architects and interior designers on office fit-outs, and so have a superb selection of functional and beautiful contemporary

Top left: this desk from **Zebrano** costs €2000 in wenge or zebrano wood.

Top right: Eames chair from **Project Office**: the ultimate desk chair.

Bottom right: part of the Bordonabe range at **Bob Bushell**.

Bottom left: Twist desk by **Nest**.

desks, comfortable chairs and modular storage. Try **Enclosure** (Southern Cross Business Park, Boghall Road, Bray, County Wicklow. Tel: 01-2765000) for a similar style.

For traditional built-in desks, shelving and storage, go to **Oakline** (8 Ranelagh, Dublin 6. Tel: 01-4977435 and Unit 1, Greenhills Business Park, Tallaght, Dublin 24. Tel: 01-4626676; www.oakline.ie). Pictured below is a corner unit in painted wood with maple contrast. Something similar will cost about €5000. Oakline designs around any space and offers many styles, finishes and woods.

No one really wants an ugly chair on wheels in a home office. How about an elegant side chair that also does desk duty? Select a chair with good spine support and be sure to stretch at regular intervals. Don't judge on looks alone; the most attractive chair might not be the best for your physique. If you choose an upholstered chair, steer clear of light-coloured fabrics: newsprint, printer toner and uncapped pens can wreak havoc in a home office. See the Dining Room section for chairs. Alternatively, the Eames chair pictured on page 108 is iconic and possibly the best 'proper' office chair you can have. It catches your back and bottom perfectly, it's sturdy and deep

enough to sit in for hours at a time and can be bought for €2240 at **Project Office** (2 Exchange Street Upper, Dublin 8. Tel: 01-6715700). Yes, I know, rather expensive.

See the lighting section: most of the shops mentioned do a variety of desk lamps. But to me the best is the Tolomeo desk lamp by Artimede, available from €170 at **Bob Bushell**. It gives really good directional light and looks great too.

Every office needs a clock. At **Peter Johnson Interiors** (Cow's Lane, Temple Bar, Dublin 8. Tel: 01-6334325) fun clocks are mounted to the wall in individual pieces. The small one costs €35; the large is €50.

Design Flow (**Unit 1B, Distillery Court, 537 North Circular Road, Dublin 7. Tel: 01-8349712; www.designflow.ie**) was set up three years ago by Robert Trench and specialises in office furniture. The products represented are (relatively) competitively priced and have real integrity (see furniture by star designer Antonio Citterio). Trench deals mostly with architects and interior designers but will also take small direct orders.

The Man Who Bought His Own Furniture

Michael Parsons

Did you fancy having a La-Z-Boy in your sitting-room? But were you worried by what your snooty architect neighbours would think of you buying a 'Rialto' recliner?

Furniture etiquette is a social minefield with endless potential for gaffes. First there was that awful U and Non-U business of 'sofa' or 'settee' from arch-snob Nancy Mitford. Then along came Alan Clark, Tory MP and celebrated diarist, who cruelly dismissed Michael Heseltine's prime ministerial ambitions with the observation that he was the kind of man 'who bought his own furniture'.

'How's your new house coming along?' ask friends, stifling yawns. There is no subject more obsessively interesting and greedily time-consuming for the proud new owner. And none more boring for the smug, 'settled' community. All eyelids except your own begin to droop as you regale company with the difficulty of tracking down the 'right' dining table or locating the 'perfect' little bookcase to fill that wasted space in the alcove.

Tastes in home furnishings have changed considerably since de Valera's Ireland when the ideal homestead was rustic and preferably located in a valley near Slievenamon. A mid-20th-century *Rural Reader* for Irish schools taught children, even urchins from inner-city slums, that 'the spacious, whitewashed kitchen of the typical Irish farmhouse is beautiful and picturesque [quite unlike, it noted coolly, 'town' kitchens] with a long old settle under the back window and strong hand-made chairs of ash with bottoms cunningly woven in rushes or in hempen cord, and backs slanting at exactly the right angle which yields perfect comfort'. Who needed Habitat?

Bedrooms had distempered walls – though dairy farmers could stretch to bordered wallpaper – a Narnia-style wardrobe, a dressing-table big enough for the cast of *La Cage aux Folles* and the kind of brass bed in which Maureen O'Hara made a quiet man of John Wayne. We've come a long way since that vale of tears and now most Irish people live in cities or large towns. Woodwork has dropped way down the school curriculum and a good cabinetmaker these days is more likely to have learnt his trade in Warsaw than in Waterford.

So off we flock to huge 'out-of-town' stores with TV studio lighting and football-pitch-sized floor displays of aspirational rooms. A single chair can cost €1,000 – but who's worried about the price? Consumers are spending like there's jam today and quince jelly tomorrow.

There is such a wealth of choice and colour and

design – with each item more tempting than the last. Furniture 'ranges' (the word 'suite' is strictly verboten these days) all seem to be named after exotic places – the 'Luxor', or the 'Barcelona', or the 'Milano'. But you never see a sofa called the 'Minsk' or an armchair called 'Pyongyang'. And just wait till Ikea opens and every single item has a dinky Swedish name – beds called 'Kritter' or 'Noresund' and coffee tables called 'Angersby' or 'Funka'.

And pretty quickly you also discover the Gulliver principle of Irish furniture shopping. While most of the 70,000-odd new 'residential units' built in the past twelve months are apparently designed for Lilliputians, most of the furniture on sale is of truly Brobdingnagian proportions. So while your kitchen is barely the width of an open copy of this book, the tables for sale could comfortably seat the Waltons for a Thanksgiving dinner or a breakfast meeting of the Cabinet.

And then you try to buy something.

'I want that one,' you say, pointing to a sleek sofa in chocolate brown carrying a price tag you'd expect on a Nissan Almera. 'Yes, it's beautiful, isn't it?' says a proud assistant, regarding it with the awe a National Museum curator reserves for the Derrynaflan Chalice.

'When could you deliver it?' 'Oh,' says the assistant, 'it takes about fourteen weeks. We have to order it from the factory.' Since you don't fancy the uncomfortable prospect of a further three-and-half wretched months watching *Desperate Housewives* seated on your mother's 'loaned' wing-back fireside chair from the Balmoral range, you make the first of many compromises. They 'could sell you the leather two-seater'. It's a 'slightly shop-soiled' display model and the colour – primrose yellow – isn't great, and won't really go with the curtains, but it is immediately available so you convince yourself that it's a bargain.

You pay a deposit and delivery is promised for next Friday ('Sorry, we don't do Saturday deliveries.').

'Between 9 and 11,' they said, so you take the morning off and settle down with Sudoku while you wait. And before you realise what time it is *Liveline* has started and the delivery man rings from the van and says he's stuck on the M50 and won't be there until 'some time' after five. And this is only the beginning. You need another bed and a locker and a coffee table and a proper kitchen table and more chairs. And don't forget the cushions! And well, quite honestly, where on earth do your friends think you would get the time to go and see *The Devil Wears Prada* and, no, you didn't hear about the awful events in the Sunni Triangle and you certainly don't have time to read *Village* magazine. After all, you've still got to get a chest of drawers, and another wardrobe and a butcher's block for the kitchen. Did you see that one in Dunnes?

Michael Parsons is a journalist with The Irish Times.

SPECIAL THINGS

SORCHA TUNNEY POSES IN FRONT OF A 19TH-CENTURY CHAIR FROM
SHARON CREAGH INTERIORS IN RATHGAR. CREAGH SELLS MOSTLY
REPRODUCTION FURNITURE BUT ALSO THE ODD ANTIQUE SUCH AS
THIS. SHE WILL ALSO RE-UPHOLSTER OLD PIECES. WHILE IN THE
DUBLIN 6 AREA, VISIT HELEN TURKINGTON, SERENDIPITY, LAMPS
& LIGHTING AND MITOFSKY.

STYLE SOURCE: DON'T BE A SNOB

A surplus of interior-design shows on TV has turned decoration into a spectator sport in which formulaic ideas are put forward as the last word in style. Whatever happened to the idea of adding your own stamp? Finding a piece of furniture that takes a room out of the ordinary should be the purpose of your visit to the shops in this section.

This doesn't always mean spending a lot of money. 'Don't be a snob – there's always something to be found in charity shops,' says interior designer Sarah Cruise. 'Find out when they redo their windows so you can be first to see the best stuff.' She recommends **Mrs Greene for Cheeverstown** in Templeogue, Dublin 6w. (Tel: 01-4924867) and **The Wheelchair Association,** Broadmeadows, Newcastle Road, Lucan, County Dublin (Tel: 01-6302479). Cruise once found a small Georgian drop-leaf table for €200. Cha Cha Seigne says: '**St Vincent de Paul** has a depot off

Gardiner Street in Dublin where people donate furniture. I like to scout around there for an old chest, a bedside locker or a table. Also look in antique shops in the country; they usually have great things that would cost a fortune in Dublin.' Fashion designer Joanne Hynes says: 'I collect glass, and charity stores are great for unusual things. In **Oxfam Home** (86 Francis Street, Dublin 8. Tel: 01-4020555 and Bray, County Wicklow. Tel: 01-2864173) I got a bowl in the shape of petals for €4 and in the **Cancer Research Shop** on Camden Street in Dublin a set of six lovely yellow glass plates for €8, which I use to hold white candles. The pleasure of looking around these shops is finding something you don't expect – some days you see nothing, others something amazing.' Occasional model Lorna Brittan agrees: 'There's nothing more relaxing than looking through junk shops. I try to think of alternative uses for the things I find. For example, I used a wrought-iron Victorian sink support as a bracket for a shelf for my microwave.'

STYLE SOURCE: THE FRENCH AND NEW ENGLAND LOOK

Glenna Lynch of **Mimosa Interiors** (Dún Laoghaire Shopping Centre. Tel: 01-2808166 and Cranford Centre, Stillorgan Road, Dublin 4. Tel: 01-2602443) is known for her clued-in decorating knowledge and, of course, the furniture she sells. Pieces inspired by New England sit cheek-by-jowl with Gustavian, Danish and French styles in her wonderfully cluttered Cranford Centre shop. She has a second shop in Dún Laoghaire but the one in Cranford Centre has better stock and a second showroom dedicated to dark-wood furniture and upholstery. A few contemporary lamps are thrown in for good measure but on the whole, Glenna says, 'Mimosa's about easy living, furniture that is light and fresh – things people might like if they want an interior that is neither entirely traditional nor entirely contemporary.' The furniture is a lot better quality than many other shops that offer a similar style: more solid and softer colours.

Top: Fashion designer Joanne Hynes shops high and low: here she examines a velvet bedspread at **Brown Thomas** but she's equally at home sifting through a charity shop.

Bottom: Cha Cha Seigne with Lorna Brittan.

Remember that what you see on the shop floor is a representation of what is in the warehouse, so ask if you are looking for something specific. Find big buys such as lovely linen sofas (from about €1500 to €2600) from France, and Aubusson-style rugs, but this is also a great place for hard-to-find things like small folding tables, traditional kitchen lighting (ceramic rise-and-fall fixtures), freestanding wood bathroom sinks and well-priced garden pieces from €195. Gustavian mirrors are about €600, console tables €300, silver-plated lamps €250 each, extendable tables €1195 and great big bookcases €1600.

Rachel Allen first told me about **Allabri**, the shop of husband-and-wife team Vicky and Stuart Andrews (The Mall, Riverside Way, Midleton, County Cork. Tel: 021-4634131). He's been making furniture for years and she has the style to pull it all together. You will find painted furniture with a shabby chic look (distressed finishes and light colours) that is a mix of Irish, French and Scandinavian style. Some pieces are old (they search out things that have potential and restore them) and Stuart makes everything else. Visit if you like traditional style but want to lighten the look of your home with furniture that isn't predictable or pretentious. Prices are reasonable: 'We try to make things that are affordable for young people,' says Vicky. 'They live in standard homes but don't want a standard interior.' There are also many small accessories, some produced locally. For example, very popular coat-hook panels are made to order from €95. There are old sideboards for about €600 that have been repaired and updated with a paint finish – they are versatile and could be used in a kitchen, hall, large bathroom or bedroom as a dressing table. Small painted iron console tables usually sell for about €80. A cute daybed with a padded seat is €475 – Nordic style with a look of the Irish settle about it.

Villa Mia is a small shop in Trim, County Meath (Tel: 046-9486717) located in a limestone-faced building that also houses owner Joan Fagan's floristry business. Fagan sells small pieces of pale-painted furniture and a

lot of table-top goods – china, cutlery, glassware, dishes and display items – as well as towels, bathroom bits and lighting. At www.villacollection.dk, you can see larger pieces that can be ordered.

Sharon Creagh (**Sharon Creagh Interiors**, 57 Highfield Road, Rathgar, Dublin 6. Tel: 01-4970731) is skilled at painting furniture with unusual effects but also does complete home overhauls. She excels at the oddest things – from a crazy-shaped headboard to a fabric cover for a birdcage. Her shop in Rathgar is home to painted wood furniture with carved decoration, bolts of *toile de Jouy* fabric, spindly wrought-iron garden furniture, soft paint shades and so on. Feminine and pretty just about sum it up. What's nice is that most of these pieces are one-offs that Creagh has customised herself. Apart from girly things, on occasion you'll find Victorian spoon-back chairs and great garden furniture, such as iron daybeds for a couple of hundred euro.

Glynis Robins and Cathy White of the **Dalkey Design Company (**20

Top: **Allabri** in Midleton, County Cork.

Bottom: a wrought-iron daybed from **Sharon Creagh Interiors**.

Railway Road, Dalkey, County Dublin. Tel: 01-2856827) were among the first to introduce the French look to Ireland. And they still do it best: what they have is the real deal, not repro. In particular see wonderfully romantic antique chandeliers (a swirl of wrought-iron and a dash of jewel-coloured glass) that Robins brings back from France; antique linen for the bed and table; and cushions and vintage glass, such as delicate platters, drinking glasses and candle-holders.

Pia Bang's taste ought to be pickled in a jar and kept for posterity. She is another person who introduced French style early on, mixed with the light-white look of her native Denmark. But her interiors shop (**Pia Bang Home,** 2 South Anne Street, Dublin 2. Tel: 01-8883777) has moved on to include a mix of Scandinavian country living and the Cape Cod look, something that seems to suit a lot of Irish tastes. The shop is spread over three floors and has furniture, soft furnishings, accessories and home gifts sourced from Belgium, Holland, France and the US. I challenge even die-hard modernists not to melt at some of her sweet things. Key features include off-white or pale-grey painted furniture alongside checked, striped or sprig-printed cotton fabrics, small chandeliers and

mirrors. My favourite is the basement area, where children's furniture and traditional toys are the cutest in town and not over-priced.

Eve Home Accessories (Meridian Point, Greystones, County Wicklow. Tel: 01-2016358) is a shop with things that are what you might call refined. Colours are mostly chalky and pale. What you'll find are small pieces of furniture that will bring lightness to your home: useful little lamps and side tables, upholstered stools and freestanding towel rails. See her antique-looking tableware and preppy checked and striped bedlinen by Lexington.

Also try: **Serendipity** (70 Rathgar Avenue, Dublin 6. Tel: 01-4968489) for more painted furniture; it's good for smaller accessories too; **Homes in Heaven** (Upper George's Street, Dún Laoghaire. Tel: 01-2802077) for hardwearing, sturdy furniture and nice kids' stuff; **French Country Interiors** (Abbey Street, Cahir, County Tipperary. Tel: 052-41187; www. frenchcountryinteriors.ie) for real French antiques, particularly beds;

Whitewood and Linen (Unit 32, Naas Town Centre, County Kildare. Tel: 045- 856482); **Quest Interiors** (37 Francis Street, Dublin 8. Tel: 01-4540299) for heavily carved painted pieces; **Thornby Hall** (Millbrook, Naas. Tel: 045-901551; www.thornbyhall. ie), is a large showroom that is strong on traditional lighting and hard-to-find things like butlers' trays and good indoor plant holders.

STYLE SOURCE: ASIAN

Those who love Asian furniture should go to **Eminence** (52 Sandycove Road, County Dublin. Tel: 01 2300193; www.eminence.ie). Owner Fiona Barron sells antique and reproduction furniture sourced on trips to China, Tibet and Mongolia. They're the kind of objects that are practical but also make a room sing. 'Part of the appeal is that they work in almost any kind of interior,' says Barron. 'They look great with contemporary furniture or antiques.' Barron opened the shop after an inspiring holiday to China. Once back in Dublin she began to educate herself about Chinese furniture. Prices are accessible: 'I want things to be within most people's reach,' she says. She handpicks the furniture at out-of-the-way markets or directly from craftspeople and takes an ethical approach, paying a fair price and safeguarding against child labour. 'It's something people want reassurance about. I'm choosing everything myself so I see how and where the new pieces are made.' Don't miss the long, scroll-legged benches that could be used as coffee tables (about €600); Chinese official red lacquer chairs (about €450); Tibetan trunks (about €700) and large Chinese cabinets that could be used for dining-room storage (about €1700).

Jennifer Goh's shop in Carrick-on-Shannon (Landmark Court, Carrick-on-Shannon, County Leitrim. Tel: 071-9622208. www.jennifergohdesign.com) is packed with the spoils of her trips to Burma, China and Tibet. Goh, who was born in Malaysia of Burmese and Chinese parents and raised in Vancouver, arrived here after meeting an Irishman in Canada. She believes her shop is popular because 'prices aren't excessive and the furniture is high quality'. She says everything is antique, not reproduction, with versatile pieces such as lacquered chests that can be used for linen, clothes or crockery (from €2500) and altar tables that can be put in a hall or behind a sofa (from €1500). It's a fun place to visit: a little treasure trove.

Becky and Conrad Byrne, the owners of **Villa & Hut** (79 Main Street, Gorey, County Wexford. Tel: 053-9481162; www.villaandhut.com) live in Indonesia for six months of the year and are agents for a line of Asian furniture that they supplement with finds of their own. Most of the furniture is from Bali and Java and they promise that everything is from fair-trade sources and that the wood comes either from reclaimed or recycled timbers. The shop offers a large range of hardwood dark furniture from beds to dining tables and smaller items such as mirrors and lamps, all in the curving style associated with the countries of origin. It's a place to find character-building blocks for a room: remember a piece or two is probably enough.

Also try: **Décor** (14a Wexford

Street, Dublin 8. Tel: 01-4759010) for charming, inexpensive chairs, tables and chests with a rough ethnic feel; **Seabourn Chic** (The Murrough Wicklow Town. Tel:, 0404-64005; www.seabournchic.com) for hand-crafted teak furniture, lighting and accessories created from recycled wood, Bali style. This company also offers a custom-made service. At **Asian Silk Road** (Unit 95, Malahide Road, Industrial Park, Dublin 17. Tel: 01-8485044). Eastern fabrics are a speciality.

STYLE SOURCE: TRADITIONAL

Interior designer Dee Brophy lived in France, New York and Brussels before returning to open **Bygone Days** in a cottage in the grounds of the Killashee House Hotel near Naas, County Kildare (Tel: 045-901251; www.bygonedays. ie). Here you will find antiques and reproduction furniture plus small items such as cushions made from vintage fabrics, old china and elegant lamps on interesting bases. Cosy, traditional-style armchairs can be ordered in various fabrics. Open Thursday to Sunday only.

While in Naas check out four other shops in particular. **SKI Interiors** (Stephenstown, Brannockstown, Naas, County Kildare. Tel: 045-442866; www.skiinteriors.com) is the place to go for fabrics by Farrow & Ball, Ralph Lauren, Cole & Son and Manuel Canovas. The shop also stocks reproductions from every period and is good for dining chairs and Japanese-style bureaux. **Interiors Bis** (The

Left: find ethnic stools like these at **Décor**.

Right: **Jennifer Goh**'s shop in Carrick-on-Shannon.

Barn, Yeomanstown, Carragh, Naas, County Kildare. Tel: 045-856385) will make upholstered furniture to order. **Renaissance Interiors** (Stone Manor House, Naas Road, Rathcoole, County Dublin. Tel: 01-4587373) is also worth a visit for traditional furniture and modern pieces. **Dwell** (M7 Business Park, Naas, County Kildare. Tel: 045-898134) is good for teak floor mats, made from small individual pieces, that cost about €200 for a large size.

Photographer Perry Ogden tipped me off about **Around the Irish House**, a venture in traditional Irish furniture set up by Joe Lennon, an antique dealer from County Louth. He is guided by American Pip Simmons who has a home in County Louth and sells the furniture at her interiors shop in the Bahamas. The country-style pieces are now available at a shop in Dromiskin, County Louth (Tel: 042-9382890). Dressers, tables, chairs, sideboards and freestanding kitchen bits are either old pieces or newly made by Lennon before being painted, 'distressed' or simply waxed. Sample prices: €450-€3,000 for a dresser; kitchen tables

from €385-€1200. Pip Simmons says, 'I'm amazed that French reproduction furniture is so popular here whereas real Irish furniture is like a pair of blue jeans – the older it gets, the better it gets. This furniture is also so much more appropriate to Irish houses and can be mixed with modern pieces.' Dromiskin is a 45-minute drive from Dublin on the M1 and the shop opens Tues–Thurs 2–5pm and Sat–Sun 9am–5pm.

Londoner Mary Jane Russell married an Irishman ten years ago and when the couple moved to Cork she opened the shop **Town & Country** (46 McCurtain Street. Tel: 021-4501468). Ellie Wylie and Anna Nichols join her to make an affable trio who run the business. They do 'traditional good taste' but with a non-fusty look. First impression is of a luxurious shop: walk in and buy whatever takes your fancy or have them put together a single room or an entire house. Visit for a marvellous selection of offbeat fabrics and sisal flooring with exaggerated weaves. Also ask about Cole's new line of wallpapers inspired by David

Hicks; Farrow & Ball's thirteen new shades of paint with batty names like Elephant's Breath; and Vaughan Lighting (traditional lighting is hard to find but this company do reproductions of old lamps). The look is less about studied decoration than about things chosen because you love them. 'It's a place where you'll find a lot of very good things under one roof,' says Cork interior designer Daphne Daunt. Two items of note: ottomans in any size from about €500; elegant garden furniture that isn't 'visually intrusive', but heavy enough not to blow over (one table and four chairs cost about €800). While you're there go next door and visit **Lynes & Lynes** Antiques (48a McCurtain Street. Tel: 021-4500982).

Maeve Ward, the soft-spoken owner of **Maison** (46 Watergate Street, Navan, County Meath. Tel: 046-9066226), a shop and interior-design practice, has classic taste and top-notch goods but she is also practical and professional. She is a godsend to those confused by decorating, although Maison may not be the best place to go to if you are looking for hard-edged modernity. Ward describes her style as 'a timeless look. It's about being comfortable, relaxed and at ease, making your home feel like a home. We'll help you pick a paint colour or do up your whole house.' Maison sells bedlinen, throws, blankets, lighting, towels and mirrors, from about €20 up to several hundred euro. Upstairs there are sample books and other paraphernalia that make up the interior design side of the business:

Left: Mary Jane Russell of **Town & Country** in Cork.

Centre: fabrics and wallpapers from **Maison** in Navan.

Right: a painted sideboard from **Fassbinder & English** in Dún Laoghaire.

Mulberry, Manuel Canovas, Osborne & Little, Nina Campbell and Zoffany. Here you will find Farrow & Ball paints. Maeve Ward also works with furniture designer John Doolin to make contemporary headboards and console tables, some of which are on display.

Visit the **Fassbinder & English** showroom (Old Fire Station, George's Place, Dún Laoghaire. County Dublin. Tel: 01-2360683; www. fassbinderenglish.com) to get an idea of the quality and style of furniture that Peter Carroll and Richard O'Toole produce to order. They began working together in America, where clients included Paul Simon. On returning to Dublin they set up in business offering high-end paint finishes. Some time later, they turned to one-off pieces of furniture designed to the client's requirements. Mostly they work to traditional styles but they are never old-fashioned. Some recent work includes achieving a subtle antique finish on bookcases, gilding on Regency-style linen presses and hand-painted details on panels of armoires.

Maud Hendricks is from the Netherlands but lives with her Irish husband and family in a redbrick house in Dublin 8, where she sells furniture and other bits and pieces (**Touchwood**, 35 Hamilton Street, off South Circular Road, Dublin 8. Tel: 01-4539711; www.touchwood.ie). Visitors are free to potter around the house and pick out whatever takes their fancy. It's an unconventional approach and 'there's a bit of everything,' says Hendricks. Some pieces are antique, others newly made. One room, for example, has a few wardrobes with a farmhouse look, on top of which are placed various types of chairs: wicker, velvet, fabric-covered and painted. Make sure you also see the large lock-up across the street, which is crammed with furniture. In particular, this is a place to visit if you prefer freestanding furniture to fitted units in a kitchen. Check out the website first.

Helen Turkington's shop (Dunville Avenue, Ranelagh, Dublin 6. Tel: 01-4125138) is a hymn to polished, rich taste. She has added a consultation room at the back, where visitors can browse through fabric books from

Cole & Son, Ralph Lauren and Colefax & Fowler. There's a wall of glassware (much of it by Alessi) and china (great chocolate colours) and bed and bath goods from the White Company. At the front of the shop are bed- and living-room sets and if you're in the market for a traditional button-back sofa or a shiny mahogany dining table, this could be the place. She's also great for small things, such as cushions and lamps.

The long-established **Enniskerry Trading Company** (The Square, Enniskerry, County Wicklow. Tel: 01-2866275) has moved away from the rustic towards something more elegant. It still caters for those who like a natural look, but the tiny shop holds more European products than before, with a more classic bent. A good reason to visit is tableware, particularly chunky Belgian glassware, raw linen tablecloths and cutlery with country-style handles. Prices are mid-range. There are pretty frosted glass bowls; big old Chinese trunks and indoor copper planters in oval, square and butter-urn shapes. Be sure to ask about some

excellent new iron-and-wood open shelving, quite different to anything else around. It's worth a trip to check this out.

Architect Maria Alice Plunkett is the creator of the **Dunsany Home Collection** of floral displays and table-top accessories, sold from her boutique at Dunsany Castle, County Meath (Tel: 046-9026202; www.dunsany.com). Each room is decorated according to its function: a dining room has a table set; a hall has a dramatic floral and porcelain display. The floral imitations are stylishly arranged in everything from metre-high Italian black-glass vases to simple centrepieces. You'll find embroidered tablecloths from Portugal, ebony-handled cutlery from France, shaved wooden mango vases from Asia and lovely glass from the Czech Republic. The collection also includes porcelain vases by her husband, Edward Plunkett.

Traditional Designs (Bushfield Ave, off Marlborough Rd, Donnybrook, Dublin 4. Tel: 01-4126055) sells a mix of period, antique and art deco reproduction furniture. You'll find things for the living room, dining room and bedroom. There are also mirrors, lighting, chandeliers and beautiful hand-made oriental rugs and floor-coverings from Iran, Tibet and China. Ask to browse manufacturers' catalogues if there's something in particular you're looking for. Prices are relatively reasonable. Traditional Designs have a second shop in County Kildare (Clane Business Park, Clane. Tel: 045-902474). Ask if you're looking for something in particular – they may have it in the Kildare shop.

Interior designer Bronagh Rowell's **Harriet's House** (60 Dawson Street, Dublin 2. Tel: 01-6777077) and 30 Blackrock Shopping Centre, County Dublin. Tel: 01-2884822) is a good source for lamps and mirrors that will sit comfortably within a traditional interior. Find big faux-fur throws, plant pots, frames, cushions and other such bits. That's the 'walk-in-and-buy' side of the business – Rowell also does complete home decoration projects, curtain-making and upholstery.

Also try: **Global Village** (Blackrock Shopping Centre, County Dublin.

Tel: 01-2835550 and Powerscourt House, Enniskerry, County Wicklow. Tel: 01-2046087; www.globalvillage. ie) for almost every kind of traditional furniture in dark and painted wood – some ethnic pieces too; **Kilkenny Interiors** (8 Dean Street, Kilkenny. Tel: 056-7762450) has the cosy country-cottage look down pat: some big pieces of furniture such as painted green dressers along with everything for the table and display.

The **Shaker Store** (Ballitore, County Kildare. Tel: 059-8623372; www. shakerstore.ie) is located in the old Quaker village of Ballitore, where you can also see a 17th-century Quaker house and a Quaker mill. The furniture is made in the US by Shaker Workshops and can be bought in kit form for home assembly or the people in Ballitore will hand-finish it for you. Everything is made on a custom basis – you specify stain and pattern. Furniture includes: rocking chairs (from €230); tables and chairs (from €800/€335); tall clocks (from €665); and night stands (from €315). My favourite is an oval coffee table with removable tray (from

€295). Lighting is also available. See pictures on page 136.

STYLE SOURCE: ART DECO

Art deco has never been more desirable, nor a sounder investment. Until recently antique dealer Niall Mullen – who began his career in the antiques trade in his family's auctioneering business in Oldcastle, County Meath – operated from a warehouse in Dublin's docklands but he now has a shop on Francis Street (**Niall Mullen Antiques**, 105 Francis Street, Dublin 8. Tel: 01 4538948). Mullen specialises in art deco and while the warehouse is still packed full of 1920s and 1930s furniture, a visit to the shop will give a taste of what's on offer. He's fitted the place out in a

way that's appropriate to the period: lots of mirrors, a black ceiling, chrome picture rails and so on. What's most in demand, he says, is dining suites. They cost a lot of money (think €30,000 upwards for a macassar ebony and amboyna wood table) but the quality is superb and resale value very high. On the other hand, you'll find plenty of (relatively) affordable items too: perhaps a Bakelite lamp with chrome shade for €1940 or a walnut writing table for €2200.

Good news – or should I say *bonnes nouvelles* – for Francophiles. As the name suggests, **French Country Interiors** (www.theantiquewarehouse. ie) specialise in pale, painted furniture – but real antiques, not reproductions. Owners Michael and Celine Kennedy

Niall Mullen deals in art deco furniture in his shop on Francis Street, Dublin.

also sell French art deco furniture and have relocated from their shop in Cahir to a warehouse on the main Dublin–Cork road. The sign reads 'The Antique Warehouse' and inside furniture is displayed in three separate categories, set out in room settings. What they have is affordable and broad-ranging.

The longest established Irish dealers in art deco furniture are **Mitofsky** (8 Rathfarnham Road, Terenure, Dublin 6. Tel: 01-4920033; www. mitofskyantiques.com). They deal in serious stuff with serious prices (think tens of thousands of euro upwards). What they consider a fair price for a dining table many would consider a fair price for a house in the country. But what they have is really exquisite and with the best provenance: glass, porcelain, earthenware, lighting and silver can all be seen, as well as bigger pieces of furniture: for example, a very fine French three-leaf lacquered screen with black lacquer and ivory inlay *circa* 1930; a commode of mahogany and macassar with fruitwood inlay and gilt bronze from the Louis Süe and André Mare Rue Du Faubourg-Saint Honore

workshop *circa* 1920. Everything is in perfect order, of course. A visit to the shop is a joy and you'll also see very good art nouveau and arts and crafts furniture.

STYLE SOURCE: 20TH-CENTURY FURNITURE

Reproductions of furniture by designers such as Le Corbusier, Eileen Gray, Charles Eames and Mies van der Rohe vary in quality and price. Janie Lazar of **Design Classics Direct** (www.designclassicsdirect.ie) is an Englishwoman married to Irish architect Peter Cully. She imports high-quality copies of 20th-century classics. Because she deals directly with Italian factories and retails online, she offers lower prices than you'll find elsewhere. Make an appointment to visit her Dalkey home to see the furniture in situ. For example, she has a version of Gray's Bibendum chair (€1395) and an Eames chair and stool set (€1850). Classic can equal clichéd, so consider less well-known pieces, and if you choose something familiar, order it in an unusual colour or fabric.

Wild Child (61 South Great George's Street, Dublin 2. Tel: 01-4755099), the vintage clothing shop, has branched into furniture and lighting. Owner William Walsh's collection includes pieces by Charles and Ray Eames, Finn Juhl, Herman Miller and Arne Jacobsen. He keeps most of his furniture in a warehouse in Wicklow (Unit W1, Wicklow Enterprise Centre, The Murrough) that is open on the first Sunday of every month. There's piles of stock and containers arrive regularly. Telephone for opening times.

As the name suggests, **20th-Century Furniture** (Tel: 01-6770679) specialises in pieces from the last century, usually with a Scandinavian or 1950s flavour. Owner Olivia Delaney operates from a concession in the **Habitat** shop (6-10 Suffolk Street, Dublin 2). She was the first to introduce this furniture to Ireland in a serious way and still has some of the finest examples.

Journalist Alanna Gallagher (alannagallagher@eircom.net) has turned dealer in mid-20th-century, art deco and modernist furniture that she imports from Argentina. Her regular shipments, personally selected, include light fixtures (including Lucite lamps, Sputnik pendants and 1970s pendulum centrepieces), bedroom suites (often with chrome bedheads

Left: **NoLita** in Carlow sells a number of Eames pieces.

Right: **Project Office** sell many famous chairs, including this one by Vitra, owned by John Mahony in Dublin. To order.

and dressing tables), glass-topped sideboards, armchairs (Jetson-style pairs), dining tables and chairs, coffee tables, shelving, office desks (steel and sycamore veneers): there's a lot on offer. In general prices range from €300 to €5000. Sales are held periodically at different locations; contact Alanna for details. She will also source any particular style of vintage furniture.

Leila Ahmedova found her career in computer science in her native Finland uninspiring and after arriving in Dublin a few years ago, she opened a shop that would bring together some of the things she loves best. It's called **Nordic Living** (57 Main Street, Blackrock, County Dublin. Tel: 01-2886680; www.nordicliving.ie) and stock includes furniture ranges from Finland and small products such as glass, ceramics and textiles. If the shop has an ethos, it's to show that there's more to Nordic design than pale, white and boring. 'In Finland it's always dark and always cold, so we're creative with colour,' says Leila. You'll find many beautiful pieces along the lines of what you might expect from Scandinavian design, but the Finnish love of colour comes through in things such as wildly-patterned Marimekko fabrics and reproductions of furniture designed in the 1930s but upholstered in bright fabrics. Furniture by Alvar Aalto is a mainstay of the shop.

NoLita mixes fashion and homewares in Carlow (Unit 2 Cathedral Close, Tullow Street. Tel: 059-9140231). Friends Suzanne Cummins and Réiltín Lacey drew on retail ideas from New York for the space. 'Look cool without trying' is the overall vibe. Cummins studied fashion in New York (the shop is named after the area of the city north of Little Italy) and worked for Louise Kennedy on her return; Lacey has a background in marketing. Their small collection of furniture is a combination of restored pieces from the 1950s and 1960s and 20th-century classics from Charles and Ray Eames. There are silk-screened quilts and cushions, blossom-etched glassware, Moroccan tea sets, coffee-table books and hand-printed blossom-motif mirrors and ceramics.

Retrospect (Cow's Lane, Temple Bar, Dublin 8. Tel: 01-6726188) sells furniture, rugs and accessories from the 1930s to the 1970s, often with a heavy emphasis on kitsch. Prices are good: for example, a 1970s nest of tables with steel frame and walnut veneer could be €250 and a classic art-deco lamp with chrome base and glass shade might sell for €120. Stock changes frequently.

STYLE SOURCE: ECLECTIC CHIC

Exoticism, glamour and drama – these words sum up the look of the **Collection** (Unit 4, St Helen's Court, Lower George's Street, Dún Laoghaire, County Dublin. Tel: 01-2147700; www.the-collection.ie). Owner Kate Connolly has developed a shop known for things such as mirrored tables, cowhide chairs, lamps with ostrich-egg bases, items of colonial and African inspiration, pieces with a nod to the 1930s such as ebony and rosewood tables, chairs inlaid with bamboo, Venetian style mirrors, white lacquered Chinese style cabinets, tin-clad chests…the mix is varied. This

Top: an Alvar Aalto trolley from **Nordic Living**.

Centre: cushions from the **Blue Door,** Naas.

Bottom: **Peter Johnson Interiors.** Note the sofa by Orior.

is a place to go for a striking element you haven't been able to find or didn't know you needed. They also do staple items such as sofas and dining tables.

Cow's Lane in Temple Bar is home to **Peter Johnson Interiors** (Tel: 01-4537088). Stylewise think personal but polished. The shop is tiny but you'll see an example of a classic sofa by Orior; cool zig-zag freestanding shelving; Swedish coffee tables; a half-dozen great dining chairs and armchairs and perhaps a sideboard or two. It opens from noon until 4 p.m. Wednesday to Saturday.

Eileen Kelly opened the **Blue Door** (21 Poplar Avenue, Naas Town Centre, County Kildare. Tel: 045-901573) with the idea of bringing something new to the area. Almost all the goods in the shop are from Sweden and have fresh colours and simple design, often based around stripes or geometric patterns. 'We focus on the "soft" end of the market. That means cushions, throws, blankets, fabrics, bedspreads and so on,' says Kelly. She is a long-time traveller to Sweden and her stock is grouped by shades of colours (amazing greens, blues and pinks), and there are some witty patterns (cute dog outlines on a blanket), natural fabrics, and reasonable prices (bedcovers €120, fabrics €21 per metre, cushion covers €20). You can buy something here as a stand-alone item but it's easy to put together a look if you wish. A bedspread and a few cushions could change a bedroom, for example, without too much expense. A lot of people come here to find things for a holiday home. It's got that casual, outdoorsy feel; you could decorate a summer table with striped placemats and napkins, or garden furniture with narrow cushions. Kelly also stocks a few pieces of Norrgavel furniture, from another Swedish company. Solid wood, painted with natural matt paints or left bare, these pieces look basic at first but are well finished. For example, a very large cupboard-style unit with deep shelves costs €1669.

STYLE SOURCE: MODERN

Rua (1 Lower George's Street, Dún Laoghaire, County Dublin. Tel: 01-2304209; www.rua.ie) is owned by

furniture designer Tom O'Rahilly. Find distinctive lighting with a nod to the 1960s. But retro it isn't: these are modern pieces that will lift any room. Prices from about €200. O'Rahilly also designs coffee tables, sideboards and display podiums, some of which can be seen in the shop. It's wonderful stuff.

Michael Haberbosch is the German behind **mimo** (Tel: 086-8593044; www.mimodesign.ie), the contemporary design e-shop that previously existed as Mimo. A while ago he closed the physical shop and transferred everything to the website. Goods are available to order, although some can be seen 'in the flesh' by apointment. mimo competes on the same level as Minima and Haus – that means high-quality, high-style furniture, often expensive. But you would be surprised at how many things are affordable: for example, a steel-frame bed called Magic is €390; the Multicylinder bedside table is €124 and the Acquamiki glass ceiling light is €192. Also look out for fun things such as Philippe Starck's Bubble Club plastic sofa for €534.

Top: Tom O'Rahilly at his shop, **Rua**.

Bottom: Ross Lewis at his shop, **Zebrano**.

Left: the look from
Minotti at **Haus**.

Centre: chairs from the
Shaker Store, Ballitore.

Right: interior shot of
the **Shaker Store.**

Zebrano (91 Francis Street, Dublin 8. Tel: 01-4548750) was opened by chef Ross Lewis of Chapter One restaurant on Parnell Square. As the name suggests, what's available is furniture made from zebrano, a reclaimed wood from West Africa with dark stripes running through a paler grain. Due to its distinctive appearance, no room could take too many items, but used with restraint, one or two will pack a punch. A square side table costs €350; a glass-top dining table and ten chairs costs €2475; a wardrobe with clever compartments is €1700; and a very large low coffee table with black glass top and leather drawers is €950.

The simpler, straight-line pieces are best.

Garrett O'Hagan has given over his **Haus** premises in Crow Street, Temple Bar, Dublin, to furniture by Italian company Minotti. The shop is about a complete look as much as individual pieces. Some prices seem ridiculous – the rather straightforward Archipenko lacquered shelving unit costs €7000 – but others are worth the money, particularly sofas and other upholstered pieces. For example, the Moor chocolate linen sofa costs €10,735: it's great quality and a dateless shape. There isn't a piece of untreated wood in the place; the look

is shiny and sleek. A walk through the shop will give you an understanding of where Italian design is at the moment. The atmosphere is dark, calm and enveloping: wonderful!

Bellissima (Distillery Road, Bandon, County Cork. Tel: 023-54740; www.bellissima.ie) was opened a few years ago by Rosemary Jones, an interior designer who started her career with Kevin Kelly before setting off for the Netherlands, where she spent time as a furniture buyer. Back in Ireland, she's going after the upper end of the contemporary furniture market – those, she says, who 'want something fabulous, but know they have to pay for it.' Jones says some of her clients fly down from Dublin; she picks them up at Cork airport and they spend an afternoon at her 5000-square-foot store. There, you can get many things under one roof: furniture, lamps, rugs and so on. The stock is set up in small room scenes, so you can see what works with what, and a terraced garden shows off outdoor furniture. Soft leather sofas with every seam saddle-stitched are big sellers – a two-and-a-

half seater costs about €2500.

Also try **Galleria** (61 South William Street, Dublin 2. Tel: 01-6744736; branches in Cork and Galway). Some stock can seem a bit OTT but they also have some nice low-key pieces, including chairs and sofas by Flexform.

Duff Tisdall (537 North Circular Road, Dublin 1. Tel: 01-8558070 and Mill Street, Dublin 8. Tel: 01-4541355; www.duff-tisdall.ie) – go to this Irish company for modern pieces that aren't overly hard-edged. Designers Arthur Duff and Greg Tisdall offer a complete service from building a structure to selecting and supplying furniture.

Frank Goodwin's **Inreda** (71 Lower Camden Street, Dublin 8. Tel: 01 4760362; www.inreda.ie) has some of the most-of-the-moment furniture in the country – it's a small shop that gives a snapshot of what's hot now.

AROUND THE HOUSE

THIS EXTENDABLE ROUND BREAKFAST TABLE FROM MINNIE PETERS IN DÚN LAOGHAIRE IS ONE OF MANY TRADITIONAL STYLES THE SHOP OFFERS. THINK HIGH-END PRICES, FROM €3500 UPWARDS. TAKE A TOUR OF OTHER INTERIOR SHOPS IN THE AREA: THE COLLECTION, FIRED EARTH, PERSONALLY YOURS, INTERIOR TOUCH, HOMES IN HEAVEN, MEADOWS & BYRNE, MIMOSA, RUA, SURFACE CERAMICS AND FASSBINDER & ENGLISH ARE ALL LOCATED IN DÚN LAOGHAIRE. DRIVE A SHORT DISTANCE FURTHER ALONG THE COAST TO SANDYCOVE TO SEE EMINENCE FOR ASIAN FURNITURE, BELLE MAISON FOR GIFTS AND FORMALITY FOR GARDEN GOODS.

Top: Bob Crowley's living room features a tapestry chair from an antique shop, a lamp created from an old print roller and a 19th-century ceiling light.

Bottom: a mesh lamp from **Brown Thomas** next to a Regency bed from **Jones Antiques** on Francis Street.

ANTIQUES AND AUCTIONS

ANTIQUES

Antiques may have lost some of their appeal but good quality well-placed statement pieces look well even in a decidedly modern interior. The Mecca for antique-lovers in Ireland is Francis Street, Dublin 8. The street offers a range of shops dealing in the sublime, if very expensive, down to bric-à-brac and collectables. Here are a few of the best:

Johnston Antiques (69–70 Francis Street, Dublin 8. Tel: 01-4732384. www.johnstonantiques.net) may be at the bottom of the street but it is tops for high-class quality furniture with an emphasis on 18th-century Irish pieces. Proprietors Paul and Chris Johnston are second-generation antique dealers and extremely knowledgeable about the finer points of quality. Items in this shop carry their imprimatur and one can be satisfied that one has not only bought an elegant piece but made a sound investment. The Johnstons

always seem to have at least one important dining table and large sets of dining chairs. Good-quality Irish and English looking glasses – never called 'mirrors' in this context – also feature. For example, an 18th-century Irish mahogany side table with original marble top has a price tag of €150,000; a rare pair of English dome-topped tea caddies with contrasting inlay may be had for €5000.

At **Michael Connell Antiques** (54 Francis Street, Dublin 8. Tel: 01-473 3898) you will find an eclectic mix of 18th- and 19th-century furniture and quirky affordable items. Connell is particularly strong on brass light fittings including those by the noted Victorian designer Benson. For example, a small desk lamp with original twisted glass shade can be had for €1250 or a large Georgian lantern for €10,000. Connell concentrates on smaller pieces of furniture such as card and Pembroke tables and always has a number of nests of tables in stock. Mixed with the furniture are decorative objects such as glass, pottery and silver, and Connell has a selection of over one hundred period walking sticks. Trips to France have yielded an impressive collection of 19th-century bronzes from some of the better-known foundries.

Visit **Esther Sexton Antiques** (51 Francis Street, Dublin 8. Tel: 01-4730909) for good 19th-century dark-wood furniture such as bookcases and display cabinets. Apart from large and important pieces, there is always a good selection of card and tea tables and Sexton is particularly strong on decorative lamps. There are usually lots of small decorative items: a pair of Irish cut-glass decanters will grace any sideboard or sometimes you will find nice pieces of silver, such as inkwells. Prices vary: a Regency breakfront bookcase of unusually small proportions may be had for €28,000 or you might consider a Regency davenport at €3900. **O'Sullivan Antiques** (43-44 Francis Street, Dublin 8. Tel: 01-4541143; www.osullivanantiques.com) is certainly the largest outlet on Francis Street (they also have a branch in New York). Theirs is an extensive collection ranging across the whole spectrum

of furniture, always the best quality
and provenance. You could find was a
19th-century brass soap rack at €150
but you might also have purchased a
large partner's desk with a price tag of
€165,000. Owner Chantal O'Sullivan
is known for an eclectic collection:
she is not afraid of buying larger
pieces such as a revolving bookcase
at a mere €65,000 or a pair of garden
urns at €50,000. It should be noted
that smaller, less expensive pieces are
available too.

Oman Antiques (20-21 South
William Street, Dublin 2. Tel: 01-
6168991) deals in Georgian, Victorian
and Edwardian furniture. They're

very good at sourcing dining tables,
sets of chairs, sideboards, display
cabinets, dumbwaiters, bookcases,
desks, wardrobes, chests of drawers
and spectacular gilt mirrors. The shop
shows a fraction of what can been seen
at their warehouses at East Wall Road
and the Naas Road in Dublin – ask to
see them by appointment.

I also like **George Stackpoole
Antiques** in Adare, County
Limerick (Tel: 061-396409). A long-
established dealer, Stackpoole is very
knowledgeable: from silver and china
through to pictures; from antique prints
to smaller items of furniture. Many of
the items have a good provenance –

this adds to their appeal (and potential resale value). For example, an 18th-century Irish dish ring may be had for €4000 or an oil and cruet set with six bottles for €1250.

Just outside Belfast, visit **McHenry Antiques** (1-7 Glen Road, Jordanstown, Newtownabbey, County Antrim. Tel: 028-90862036). Ann McHenry and her son Rupert collect antiques with a very discerning eye and stock pieces of good quality that are always restored sympathetically. Furniture and other objects from Northern Irish properties tend to be just a little bit different. For example, a bow-fronted Irish mahogany side cabinet with unusual cross banding was priced at €6000 and they were seeking €28,000 for a large mahogany glass-fronted bookcase.

Apart from the shops mentioned above, be sure to visit the **Irish Antique Dealers Fair** which takes place every September in the RDS, and the Dublin and International fairs held, respectively, just before Christmas and in March, also in the RDS. You will find the best of what antique shops around the country have to offer, as well as seeing furniture from dealers who do not have shops. Dealers tend to be generous in sharing their knowledge. Make friends with them and do not be afraid to ask. They have exercised their judgement in selecting the pieces and will have avoided obvious mistakes, though they will admit that they make mistakes of their own. Different dealers have different interests and strengths. Remember to haggle. It is part of the fun and dealers never expect to get the ticket price.

AUCTIONS

There are two kinds of auctions: one offers fine antiques and the other ordinary items that are not of such good quality but perhaps more suitable to general household use. In the first category are places such as **James Adam & Sons** (26 St Stephen's Green, Dublin 2. Tel: 01-6760261); **HOK**'s showroom in Blackrock, County Dublin (Tel: 01-2885011) and **Mealys** (Castlecomer, County Kilkenny. Tel: 056-4441229). Keep an eye on the Fine Art pages of *The Irish Times* every Saturday for upcoming auctions.

Buying at one of these may be less expensive than from an antique dealer, but although you are making a saving – say €12,000 rather than €16,000 – they're really not for those on a budget. More price-friendly places include **Adams** of Blackrock, County Dublin (Tel: 01-2865146) and **Herman Wilkinson** in Rathmines (Tel: 01-4972245; www.hermanwilkinson.ie). Fashion designer Helen Cody was once a frequent visitor at Herman Wilkinson in Rathmines: 'I used to go there years ago when I had just bought my house, hadn't a bean to my name but wanted interesting things. They have the oddest stuff but can be really good for 1930s furniture. You'll pick up a big old kitchen table for a couple of euro. It's also great fun for people-watching.' Also try **Buckleys** in Sandycove (Tel: 01-2300193), **Dennis Drumm** in Malahide (Tel: 01-8452819) and **Sheppards** in Durrow, County Laois (Tel: 057-8736123). **Town & Country** (Tel: 01-8727401) on Dublin's Lower Ormond Quay organises auctions for house contents sales. Phone them to find out dates for upcoming sales.

What you should be looking for at these auctions are simple things: tables, a set of chairs (odd chairs go very cheaply and the right selection can look great around a table), chunky kitchen dressers or chests of drawers. Think everyday things that don't cost the earth but remember to examine the piece you have your eye on properly and consider how much money and time it's going to take to make any repairs. However, if all you want is an inexpensive, reasonably attractive, solid piece it hardly matters.

DOYENNE OF THE IRISH ANTIQUES WORLD ROXANE MOORHEAD SHARES HER TIPS ON BUYING ANTIQUES

1. 'To learn a lot quickly, try taking one of the many night courses around the country. The Institute

of Professional Auctioneers and Valuers (Tel: 01-6785685) do one in Dublin. The old way to learn used to be directly from an antique dealer, so always ask questions when you visit an antique shop.'

2. 'Build a relationship with a good dealer. Then, if you see something you like, don't be afraid to ask the dealer if you may bring it home to see it in context. This is not possible at auction – once you've bought, there's no going back. Today people like the thrill of auctions and the idea of getting something at a good price. But they don't get a chance to look at the piece properly and don't realise that the cost of repairs has become very expensive.'

3. 'No matter how beautiful something may be, unless you are super-rich and buying solely for investment, buy only what suits your home: you have to live with it after all. Buy one good thing once or twice a year. A lot of people want their home fitted out in one go now, but when I started out even the very well-off bought slowly. That way you can buy better quality pieces and consider what you need or want. If you can't find what you're looking for, tell the dealers about the piece of furniture you have in mind. All dealers keep a list of things people want to buy and will call you if they find it. You are under no obligation to buy.'

4. 'Make sure you know the provenance of the piece. If a dealer is in the Irish Antique Dealers Association, he or she is obliged to give a receipt stating the date and where it came from. This gives you a comeback. Be aware that furniture in overly good condition can be a giveaway with regard to authenticity. With a dining table and chairs, make sure all the leaves are original. This can be difficult to tell as old wood can be used to remake them. Make sure the wood in the tabletop has the same grain and colour as the base and legs. Dining chairs are a minefield

– legs, stretchers or backs are often replaced, and a good dealer should tell you immediately.'

Contact Roxane Moorhead at **Jones Antiques** (65-66 Francis Street, Dublin 8. Tel: 01-4546626).

Being kind to the environment and supporting an Irish product is doubly virtuous. Malone's Home Care products make wood cleaning and polishing products. I love their liquid wax in a trigger-spray bottle. Others products clean floors but contain no solvents; the ingredients are castor oil, natural caramel dyes and lavender flakes. Available at Dunnes Stores, Tesco and Londis Stores countrywide.

FLOORING

CARPETS

Spend what you can afford. A carpet takes the heaviest wear of anything in the home. Explain to the shop assistant exactly what you need and how much wear the carpet must be able to take to deal with two cats, a dog, three children or whatever.

That said, inexpensive materials such as cork, linoleum, sisal or white tiles are great if used in the right way. For example, cork tiles can be bought at **Woodies DIY** (branches countrywide) for €12 a square metre and are perfect for a small kitchen or bathroom. Inexpensive carpets are great if you're in a transitory space, such as a rented apartment. Go to **Des Kelly** (branches countrywide; www.deskellycarpets.ie) where you'll find neutral-coloured carpets, such as white carpet tiles that you could replace often because they're so cheap.

'My mother told me to use double underlay – it makes the carpet feel much thicker so your feet really sink in,' says Lisa Duffin of Bottom Drawer at Brown Thomas. She buys at **Grange Carpet & Bedding** (Deansgrange, County Dublin. Tel: 01-2896600).

Arnotts (Henry Street, Dublin 1. Tel: 01-8050400) stocks two brands, Ryalux and Causeway, which will produce carpets to your colour specifications: bring a fabric or paint sample to the store and they can match the colour. Both companies allow you to buy the

exact width you require rather than the standard sizes (so less waste). Also at Arnotts see the Chameleon line from Ulster Carpets – it lets you design your own carpet from a range of patterns and colours.

Several interior designers have mentioned **Martsworth** (Ashford, County Wicklow. Tel: 0404-40113), a furniture and carpet showroom. Reports say they fit the carpet when they say they will, don't waste time and do the job extremely well. A large range of carpets is in stock and can be laid two weeks after ordering but often considerably sooner.

William Free (Meadowbrook Mews, Ballinteer Road, Dublin 16. Tel: 01-6684763) is an excellent small carpet showroom used mostly by those in the trade. It has everything, including hard-to-find colours such as differing shades of greys. Go here for carpets that will fit right into your Tom de Paor or Boyd Cody house.

Fashion carpets are all about unusual textures. The most popular look at the moment is neutral grey or stone colours with exaggerated

Top: sisal flooring looks good initally but is very hard to keep clean.

Bottom: Lisa Duffin in her living room with double underlay carpet.

AROUND THE HOUSE

loops of wool that mimic pebbles. Try **O'Hagan Design** (102 Capel Street, Dublin 1. Tel: 01-8724016) for a good selection.

V'soske Joyce (Oughterard, County Galway. Tel: 091-552113) are well known for custom-made carpets incorporating any colours or designs you fancy. Prices start at between €250 and €300 per square metre.

Ulster Carpets are the longest-established carpet manufacturer in Ireland and are well known for their high-quality weaves in more than three hundred colours. While some patterned carpets tend towards the traditional, over the past few years the range has been updated with modern colours – look for shades of putty and very subtle checks. The company's recent collaboration with Cath Kidson resulted in colourful stripes and her signature bright florals. See www.ulstercarpets.co.uk for stockists countrywide.

Also try: **TC Matthews Carpets** (Greenhills Road, Walkinstown, Dublin 12. Tel: 01-4503822); **Glen O'Callaghan Carpets** (131b Slaney Road, Dublin Industrial Estate, Glasnevin, Dublin 11. Tel: 01-8601849); **Kevin Kelly Interiors** (Morehampton Road, Donnybrook, Dublin 4. Tel: 01-6688533).

Below: wood flooring by **Ebony & Co**.

WOOD FLOORS

Companies such as **Scotts** (124 Lower Baggot Street in Dublin. Tel: 01-6625680) will supply high-quality new parquet flooring. If you want the look of a parquet floor that is naturally aged, you need old wood blocks. The **Dublin Architectural Salvage Company** (Tel: 01-4734368) sells reclaimed parquet blocks (usually from schools, churches or convents) in oak, mahogany and teak, at €30-40 per square yard. The **Victorian Salvage & Joinery Company** (South Gloucester Street, Dublin 2. Tel: 01-6727000) also sells old parquet floors.

Two places that do mid-quality and mid-price wood floors are **Signature Wood Flooring** (Tel: 01-4299455: www.signaturewoodfloors.ie) and **Wide Plank Floors** (Unit 2-5 Albany Business Park, Kilcoole Industrial Estate, County Wicklow. Tel: 01-2760021). You might think of using this quality of flooring in secondary rooms.

Interior designer Karen Stafford (karen@renovate.ie) recommends Woodworkers (Harold's Cross, Dublin 6. Tel: 01-4901968) for French marine pine floors (matt finish) that look good but are not expensive.

John O'Rahilly of **Classic Floors** (Unit B4, KCR Industrial Estate, Dublin 12. Appointment only. Tel: 01-4924944) works with great-quality woods and does speciality finishes, wide plank and parquet but he's still a well-kept secret: Classic Floors have won various prizes for wood innovation.

In Cork, Beth Haughton of the Beth fashion store in Douglas recommends **Sean O'Neill** (Tel: 087-2925114) to lay hardwood floors. 'He laid the floors in my own home and is methodical and a perfectionist. There's an honesty there too – he won't do something that won't work.'

Ebony & Co (39 Fitzwilliam Street Upper, Dublin 2. Tel: 01-6690970; www.ebonyandco.com) supply wood floors (cherry, walnut, maple, cypress and so on) such as those that have been used in the homes of Bill Clinton, Donna Karan, Harrison Ford and Woody Allen. They're also in the Mercer Hotel in New York. Irish clients include John Rocha and Louis Walsh.

One of the things that initially set Ebony apart was that their planks are twenty-two inches wide and sixteen feet in length, which makes for a sleeker-looking floor with fewer joints. Many other companies now offer wide planks but Ebony has moved on to treating woods and using old, recycled woods. I like the rougher, natural ones best, such as 'antique branwood', used in the Dublin home of restaurateur Christian Stokes. Another nice one is Grandpa's Floor which is a recycled heart pine timber, buffed and scuffed to give a naturally aged look. Needless to say, it's all fairly expensive.

Stone and Tile

Want the smooth, cool floors of an 11th-century French abbey in your kitchen? Or the rustic stone walls of a small farmhouse in Provence? Here are a few places to try: **Artefaction** (12-13 Lime Street, Dublin 2. Tel: 01-6776495) have stone and marble pieces made to order; **Lomac Tiles** (North Wall Quay, Dublin 1. Tel: 01-8551588) specialise in porcelain tiles; **Mosaic Assemblers** (Unit 14, The Courtyard, Fonthill Industrial Estate, Dublin 22. Tel: 01-6267669 have a huge range of mosaic tiles and will create any pattern to order; **Regan Tile Design** (2 Corrig Avenue, Dún Laoghaire, County Dublin. Tel: 01-2800921) do natural stone flooring and interesting man-made alternatives; **Kilkenny Tile Store** (7 Irishtown, Kilkenny. Tel: 056-7763099). For other ideas see the bathroom section: most companies listed offer tiles.

A rubber floor is smooth, hard-wearing and can be had in almost any colour you wish. The RIAI (Royal Institute of the Architects of Ireland; www.riai.ie) recommends **Gerflor** (Carrickmacross, County Monaghan. Tel: 042-9661431; e-mail: gerflorirl@gerflor.com) as a supplier of rubber floors.

Curtains

Windows determine how you look out on to the world and also set the mood for how you feel within a room. The moulding, the view, the shape and the way light filters through – all these

elements are affected by the window treatment you choose.

'Always have curtains interlined (raw, pure cotton between the fabric and the ordinary lining) – it will make them fuller, more dramatic and let them drape better,' says interior designer Maeve Ward of **Maison** in Navan (Tel: 046-9066226). She stocks a wide range of quality fabrics by names such as Mulberry and Osborne & Little, but says: 'It's better to go for a cheaper fabric and have it interlined than an expensive one with ordinary lining.'

READY-MADE CURTAINS

If you need to cover a window today and don't have a lot of money to spend, **KA International** (Main Street, Blackrock, County Dublin. Tel: 01-2782033 and Jervis Shopping Centre, Dublin 1. Tel: 01-8781052; branches also in Cork, Galway and Enniskerry; see www.kainternational.ie for details) has some of the best ready-made options – heavy, natural linens that come in three widths, costing from €115, with either a looped or pleated

Top: gauzy fabric dresses a window but allows light into a room.

Bottom: ready-made curtains from **KA International.**

Top: fans of fabric shop **Murphy Sheehy** include fashion designer Kate O'Brien (pictured with bolts of fabric from the store)

Bottom: Tae Kwon Do champion Nicola McCutcheon used **Murphy Sheehy** ticking fabric on padded window shutters.

top. All curtains are three metres long but can be taken up by cutting the fabric and using an iron-on strip to make a hem. KA also sells lining and curtain poles, from €45, and has a call-out service to drill the pole in place. **Hickeys Fabrics** (branches countrywide. Tel: 01-2845079 for details) sell kits to make Roman blinds in different widths, costing from €45. The drop on each blind is 2.4 metres, but this can be adapted. If you're adept at putting things such as flatpacks together it's not too hard, but then you will need to get the fabric panel made up. Hickeys will do this for you but it can take ten days. Instead find someone handy with a sewing machine and ask them (nicely) to do it for you. Cut the fabric to size and sew lining behind it, before attaching the whole thing to the frame. Perhaps not quite good enough for a principal room but fine elsewhere.

Unusual curtains can be created from inexpensive six-metre-long Indian saris, which can be bought from stalls in the Market Arcade on South Great George's Street. Dublin 2.

The writer Colm Tóibín has curtains made from a rich blue sari with gold detail in the kitchen of his Dublin home. If all else fails and you are on really a tight budget, go to the **Curtain Exchange** (Adelaide Court, Albert Road, Glenageary, County Dublin. Tel: 01-2304343) for second-hand curtains. You could be in luck and find something perfect that will cost you next to nothing.

CURTAIN-MAKERS

Curtains can be a big investment so having them made properly means they last a lifetime. **Karri Stephenson** (Tel: 01-6680398) is the doyenne of curtain makers in Ireland. She has been in business since 1995 and her team of seamstresses and fitters can achieve any look (and will even hand-smock pleats). Whether the approach is classic or contemporary, she takes the view that instead of being hidden behind a torrent of fabric, windows should be cleverly enhanced, letting in light and air. Stephenson also sells fabric from her showroom, thus offering a complete service. Her tip: pure silk

is relatively inexpensive yet looks luxurious. **Margaret Buggy** (Tel: 059-9159981) is a name I had to prise from fabric distributor Gerry Cremins of **Cremins Moiselle** (The Design Centre, Bray South Business Park, Killarney Road, Bray, County Wicklow. Tel: 01-2042848; www.creminsmoiselle. com). Buggy's workroom in Ballon, County Carlow employs fifteen people and this means a fast turnaround for smaller jobs. Finished curtains should be ready about one week after you give her fabric and dimensions. What's unusual is that such efficiency does not mean that finish is compromised – details are hand-sewn and fabrics interlined. Buggy works with many of the country's better-known decorators. She also uses the best linings and eyelets and has been making curtains for thirty years. Curtain maker **Angela Lee** (Tel: 01-4902307) works in Rathgar but mostly only for interior designers, so you may have to wait a bit. You will also have to supply her with fabric. Lee herself recommends **Sharon Dunne** of the Linen Berry in Maynooth (Tel: 01-6293094) as an excellent curtain maker. In Limerick, fashion commentator Celia Holman Lee suggests **BL. Curtains Direct** (Tel: 061-355974; 087-2058514) because 'they give a great service – visiting your home and seeing what will work with what you already have. The finish is excellent.' Helen O'Connor's shop, the **Curtain and Gift Traders** (Newtown Park Avenue, Blackrock, County Dublin. Tel: 01-2836547) is good for traditional curtains and simple blinds. Their prices are reasonable and they have a selection of fabrics from which to choose.

THE BEST CURTAINS ARE ALL ABOUT CAREFUL FITTING AND FABRIC CHOICE. HERE ARE A FEW IDEAS:

Measure your window and also the distance from the top of the opening to the floor if the curtains are going to fall that far (and they almost always should: short curtains look mean). Measure the space between the top of the window and the ceiling: this could affect what kind of pelmet or pole you can have. Are there any obstructions on either side of the window? Is there a radiator underneath? Measure how far it comes out from the wall – you don't want curtains bulging over it. These things will affect the amount of fabric required and therefore the price.

Decide whether you want to buy your own fabric or try a company that offers a complete service – fabric, design, making and fitting. Make clear at the start how much you want to spend. For curtain fabrics, curtain-maker Angela Lee recommends **Murphy Sheehy** (14 Castle Market, Dublin 2. Tel: 01-6770316); **KA International**, the **Natural Interior** in Mill Street, Dublin 8 (Tel: 01-4737444), and **Form & Line** in Ranelagh, Dublin 6 (Tel: 01-4911201). This last shop is best for fabrics with a minimal bent, i.e. simple high-quality German fabrics that you won't find anywhere else. You will see moirés, oriental-style jacquard and semi-transparent fabrics. **Casa** in Blackrock, County Dublin (Tel: 01-2805805) will help you choose a fabric from their vast collection. They are best for traditional curtain styles. Owner Bernie Cassidy recently fitted out the windows of the Conrad Mount Juliet in Kilkenny. She sells brands such as Fischbacher and Robert Allen. Another recommendation from Beth Haughton of fashion store Beth in Cork is interior designer **Daphne Daunt** (Tel: 021-4357891) for her subtle, elegant style. 'She has worked on some of the most beautiful, understated houses in Cork. She's a perfectionist and the fabrics she uses for curtains are the best.' Daunt's clients include Ballymaloe House.

Blackout blinds are far better than blackout lining, which can deform the curtain shape and darken light fabrics. Try **Hickeys Home Focus** (Tel: 01-8208390) for reasonably priced blackout blinds.

Does your room face south or west? A sunny room means that deeper curtain colours will fade faster. Install a roller blind – if not, choose a lighter fabric. When choosing patterned fabrics consider whether the design will have enough repeats: a big pattern needs a big window to show it off best.

Buy a good-quality curtain pole. 'Expensive poles can be very forgiving,' says designer **Greg Kinsella** (Tel: 01-2860567): 'If you use a cheap fabric, accessorise with expensive tiebacks. Try to keep colours neutral, as they will appear a little more expensive.'

Ask how well the fabric will drape. Many people like to have it 'puddling' on the floor. Silk/viscose velvet pooled on the floor will accentuate the great flop factor of this cloth. At the top, goblet pleats can be created with tape that shapes the fabric into soft cylinders. Lining is not necessary, as this is about keeping it simple and letting a wonderful fabric do its thing.

Always bring sample books or fabric swatches home to see how they look in your room in daylight and artificial light. If colour scares you, go neutral and use colour elsewhere in the room – lamps, rugs and cushions can be easily changed. Suede and leather-eyelet curtains, opulent interlined silks and sheer fabrics are in vogue.

Shutters are an alternative to curtains: **Benedicts** (Avondale Hall, Carysfort Avenue, Blackrock, County Dublin. Tel: 01-2881693) supply and fit plantation-style shutters, good for bathroom windows. I think they have the best selection.

Fabrics, Paints and Wallpaper

You'll find a great selection of fabrics, wallpapers, trimmings, blinds and carpet samples at the **Interior Library** (6 Shelton Drive, Kimmage Road West, Dublin 12. Tel: 01-4059856), a shop opened by decorator Lucinda Batt, whose clients include Sir Anthony O'Reilly. She has put together a collection of the above, with varying styles and prices in mind. However, Batt believes that a house should not look obviously decorated, and this sets the tone for much of what's available.

Bring an interior designer with you to the fabric showrooms of **Cremins Moiselle**. Owners Louis Moiselle and Gerry Cremins deal only with the trade. Set aside most of a morning or afternoon – the range is varied and extensive and a visit can prove, well, a bit of a head trip. This is high-quality stuff, with styles ranging from chintzy to cool. While fabric hunting in Bray, visit **Material World** (Church Terrace, Bray. Tel: 01-2866668).

Town & Country (46 McCurtain Street, Cork. Tel: 021-4501468) has a marvellous selection of offbeat fabrics (also ask about Cole's new line of wallpapers inspired by David Hicks). The shop stocks Raoul Textiles – amazing quality with beautiful faded subtle patterns – but terribly pricey: 'More expensive than hard-core drugs,' comments one fan, tongue firmly in cheek. Think upwards of €95 a metre. 'They fit in well with an existing scheme because they're not too new-looking or commercial,' says Mary Jane Russell, one of the three women behind the business. Her sister, Katherine Ireland, works in LA creating soft understated fabrics in beautiful colours. Again expensive, from €84 per metre. The shop has reasonably priced fabrics too, for example striped Swedish cottons at €25 a metre.

Patricia Tyrrell of **Fabrique Interiors** (The Cottage, Main Street, Dunshaughlin, County Meath. Tel: 01-84211716 www.fabrique.ie) makes all sorts of things – blinds, curtains, footstools, bolsters, headboards and loose sofa covers – from fabrics the company supplies (prices start at €10 per metre). Finish and detailing are excellent.

Also try the following for curtain fabrics, upholstery fabrics and wallpapers: **Interior Touch** (67 Convent Road, Dún Laoghaire, County Dublin. Tel: 01-2809044; www.interiortouch. ie); **SKI Interiors** (Stephenstown, Brannockstown, Naas, County Kildare. Tel: 045-442866, www.skiinteriors. com) for fabrics by Farrow & Ball, Ralph Lauren, Cole & Son and Manuel Canovas; **Jenkins Interior Design** (The Square, Cavan. Tel: 049-4331151) stocks fabrics by Sanderson, Jane Churchill, Robert Allen and offers a curtain-making and fitting sevice as well as American-style wood shutters and blinds; **Benedicts**; **Brian S. Nolan** (102 Upper George's Street, Dún Laoghaire. Tel: 01-2800564); **Bushfield Interiors** (Dunleer, County Louth. Tel: 041-6851028); **Porter Ryle** (Trafalgar Square, Greystones, County Wicklow. Tel: 01-2016379) stock Cole & Son wallpapers, Farrow & Ball paints, Mulberry, Colefax & Fowler and Liberty fabrics. **Castle Curtains & Blinds** (1a Three Rock Road, Sandyford Industrial Estate, County Dublin. Tel: 01-2955100); **Kevin Kelly Interiors**; and **Angela O'Connor** (9 Leopardstown Avenue, Blackrock, County Dublin. Tel: 01-2888811) are all worth a visit.

Left: red damask wallpaper from **Dunnes Home**, part of a range that starts at €20 per roll. It is washable, with a vinyl finish. The lamp is by Santa & Cole at **Duff Tisdall**.

Centre: fabrics from **Cremins Moiselle in Bray**.

Right: wallpaper from **Maison** in Navan.

Top: one of my favourite grey paints is Antimony matt emulsion by Kevin McCloud for **Fired Earth**

Bottom: fashion designer Aideen Bodkin painted her bedroom walls with Wine Damson paint by Colour Trend at **MRCB** and used gold paint by the same company to paint lotus flower patterns.

SPECIALIST WALLPAPER

David Skinner Wallpaper (www. skinnerwallpaper.com) is a small company making traditional hand-printed wallpapers. Wrap a wall with a design from its Great Houses of Ireland line, a collection of wallpapers reproduced from original designs found in Georgian houses. Think delicate but vivid. All are available in a range of stock shades and custom colours; prices start at about €100 a roll. The company also conserves wallpaper – recent projects include the restoration of Lissadell House in County Sligo. Tom Watts of **Imagine Wallpaper** (Mall House, Thomastown, County Kilkenny. Tel: 056-7724760; www.imaginewallpaper.com) has developed a system of producing digital wallpaper which can be printed in panels approximately one metre wide. The company will accurately reproduce from photographs, paintings or illustrations and create wallpaper using these images. Their wall covering is rich in colour with an amazing texture and virtually indestructible in

the most testing of environments. It may be wiped clean and is printed to a resolution suitable for close inspection. Clients include the Merrion Hotel.

WALL PAINT

PAINTERS

Light colours are often used in period homes as an alternative to traditional dark shades and few have done this better than Louise Kennedy in Merrion Square. Under her direction, Robbie Keating and David Smullen of **Purple Ark** (Tel: 087-6424166) painted her home and store in various off-white colours. Purple Ark is a specialist paint company that often works with older buildings and paints everything from furniture and chandeliers to murals and gilding. Apart from perfect finish (and reliability) they are particularly good at mixing paints, which they did for Kennedy. 'We made warm whites that avoid a clinical look.' says Keating. "Because most of the rooms in Louise Kennedy's house have different quality of light, different shades of white were needed. The floor – carpets or wood – also affect the shade that should be

used.' My own favourite shade of white is Sensitive White by Colour Trend: it's not too stark. Another painter I have heard great things about is **Michael Davidson** (Tel: 087-6645248) who devotes a lot of time to preparation, leading to very good results. Interior designer Laura Farrell recommends painter **Tony Kampf** (Tel: 01-8214517). Incidentally, speaking of wall treatments, Farrell's company **Scudding Clouds** (www.scuddingclouds.com) specialises in Japanese plasters that give a silky, lush effect, with materials such as straw included in the mix. They can be mixed in almost any colour. Make an appointment to visit Laura Farrell's studio in Dublin city centre.

SHOPS AND RANGES

The shop that offers most is **MRCB Paints** (12–13 Cornmarket, Dublin 8. Tel: 01-6798755; Maynooth Road, Celbridge, County Kildare. Tel: 01-6303666; and Tramore Road, Waterford. Tel: 051-351299). Visit the branch on Conrmarket and you'll find a new shop dedicated solely to Farrow & Ball paint next door (Tel: 01-

6770111). Some may snigger at the ubiquity of their French Grey shade but it's very versatile on walls and furniture, combining easily with other colours. What's great about this shop is that you can see the paint ranges displayed on walls and not just from a tiny chart. Cheap, watery paint is never worth buying, so spend money. Paint that doesn't cost quite as much as some other brands, but still provides good quality and a decent colour range, is the General Paints Professional Range at MRCB. Five litres costs €40. Another nice one is Dulux's Moda range. There are fifteen colours, all designed to work with one another – good for

those who lack confidence choosing colours – so it's hard to go terribly wrong. Colours range from creams and yellows to powdery pinks and blues. Interior designer Lisa McNulty designed the collection. It costs from €36 for 2.5 litres at shops countrywide. **Fired Earth** (31 Lower Ormond Quay, Dublin 1. Tel: 01-8735362 and 20 Lower George's St, Dún Laoghaire, County Dublin. Tel: 01-6636160) also has a lovely (and extensive) selection of their own-brand paints. Grey is a great neutral for walls. I like Antimony matt emulsion by Kevin McCloud for Fired Earth (€33 for 2.5 litres). Meanwhile, Crown's Easy Clean is a tough paint

range for walls, wood and metal:
a good one for children's rooms or
kitchens, it is available at DIY stores
countrywide. It's worth noting that
AuroKlee Paper (89 North Circular
Road, Dublin 7. Tel: 01-8383544) sells
totally organic and solvent-free paints,
great for asthmatics and people with
allergies. DeVine Paints are an offshoot
of the Irish company Colour Trend and
have a sophisticated range of colours,
including a good range of strong gutsy
shades. There are both water-based and
oil-based paints and these are available
at **MRCB**.

SPECIALIST PAINTERS

Painting walls is the easiest form
of decoration. For those who want
something unusual (but not rag-
rolling or sponging) go to paint-effect
and mural specialist **Peter Sutton
Fitzgibbon** (Mountjoy Studios, 27
Mountjoy Square, Dublin 1. Tel: 087-
2503140; www.decorativepainting.
net). **Christopher Moore** (Tel: 087-
2500380) is another talented paint
specialist. He can create almost any
effect but what I like best is his ability

to age walls, to take them down a
notch so they look older and give them
a subtle tinge of colour.

**David Hicks was the English designer who
shook up the staid decoration of 18th- and
19th- century houses in the 1960s, using
geometric prints and mixing pop art with
Chippendale. Hicks, pictured left in 1970
with his wife Pamela Mountbatten, painted
the walls of his own living room black (note
the black carpet too). It worked because
the walls had an almost lacquered sheen,
so black reflected the light rather than
soaking it up. The best paint to achieve
something similar is Colour Trend's Alkyd
Gloss, available at most hardware shops.
But walls first need to be prepared with an
alkali-resistant primer and an undercoat
before applying the heavy oil-based gloss.
For small areas such as architectural details
or even a fireplace, use Jap Black (also by
Colour Trend), a Japanese lacquer that gives
a very smooth mirrored finish.**

LIGHTING

If you are doing up your home from scratch, lighting should be a priority. It is worth getting a floor plan to scale, marking out where your furniture might go and planning lighting around that. There are four obvious lighting options – wall, ceiling, floor and table. You will need to mark where lights, sockets and switches are needed. Do this with your interior designer or architect. For floor lamps, consider fitting sockets in the floor itself to reduce the length of flex needed.

If you want to get really serious, a lighting designer will help you do all this (but don't step on the toes of your architect or interior designer). Dublin-based **David Bain** (Tel: 087-2584190) is good, because what he does is never obvious but always enhances atmosphere. A lighting designer sounds very grand but it's just about helping you choose lighting that works in a particular room. Bain deals with a large range of good-quality fittings, will install everything and is not as expensive as you might imagine. He has installed lighting in Áras an Uachtaráin. Rocky Wall of **Wink Lighting** (Tel: 01-2836700 www.wink.ie) also comes with good recommendation, as does **Donegan Lighting Design Partnership** (Tel: 01-6705022).

When Cathy Berry worked in London for a lighting consultancy company, her clients included rock stars and galleries. After returning to Dublin ten years ago, she set up her own company (**Aurora Lighting Design & Supply.** Tel: 01-4549837; 086-2512415). 'At that time lighting was still an afterthought in interior design concepts,' she says. 'Now I work a lot on high-end homes. I meet clients and discuss concept, then we do a complete CAD lighting layout for the electrician. Fittings are sourced around Europe and we do site visits to ensure everything is running to plan.' Cathy is the main lighting design consultant for all Smarthome proposals.

Whatever else you do, always use a qualified electrician. Never attempt electrical work yourself. In Cork, for electrical jobs call **Andy Dowling** (Tel:

Top: a simple paper
shade hung low
creates a focal point.

Bottom: David Loughane
of **Minima** sits on a
cube light from **Muji**.
A bulb lights from
within. It can be used
as a seat or a table and
costs around €150.

021-4963469). He's someone who just
comes in and sorts out the problem.

LIGHT FITTINGS

LOW PRICE

Not flying to Tokyo this year? Enjoy
the simplicity of Japanese design with
round paper shades from **Stock** (33
South King Street, Dublin 2. Tel: 01-
6794317) from about €6, or similar
from most DIY shops, such as **Woodies**
and **B&Q** (countrywide). They are best
hung very low, as pictured left. At this
level a paper shade can be a reading
lamp, create a warm focal point and
change from a simple element into a
design detail.

You sometimes see great old lamps
at fairs and auctions. But what makes
a good deal? Don't worry about the
condition of the cord – an electrician
should rewire anything you buy
second-hand, so you know it is safe.
Lamps from the 1960s and 1970s
often offer character and good value.
Add a dimmer switch: it will cost only
about €20. Keep an eye out for light
fixtures from old office buildings, such
as desk lamps, or oversized hanging

Top: embellished paper shades from **Peoba** in Dundalk.

Bottom: desk light, available at **Bob Bushell,** used here as a bedside light.

fixtures that might have been used in hotel or theatre lobbies – perfect for a hall or stairwell or even above a dining table. For new lighting, try **B&Q**: antique-look fixtures and 1930s styles for €30-€50. **Dunnes Home** (South Great George's Street, Dublin 2, Cornelscourt, Dublin 18, and large Dunnes Stores branches countrywide) is always good for inexpensive lamps. Also try **Hicken Lighting** (17 Lower Bridge Street, Dublin 8. Tel: 01-6777882).

MID PRICE

The **National Lighting Centre** (Upper Erne Street, Dublin 2. Tel: 01-676 9555) is a one-stop shop: you're sure to find something. **Willie Duggan Lighting** (Rose Inn Street, Kilkenny. Tel: 056-7764308; www. willieduganlighting.com) has some of the most cutting-edge lamps in the country – worth a drive from Dublin. Duggan is also a lighting designer and one of the best. **Mobilia** (Drury Hall, Lower Stephen's Street, Dublin 2. Tel: 01-4780177) is good for simple drum-shade lamps for about €200.

The Bestlite lamp, at **Nordic Living** (57 Main Street, Blackrock, County Dublin. Tel: 01-2886680) is minimalism with history. It's the real deal and will add gravitas to any room. Designed in the 1930s, it is probably one of the most copied lamps ever. The light channelled through the metal shade is very focused – this is a task light, not for lighting a whole room. Prices range from about €500 (see website for picture). It's also sold at **Brown Thomas** (Grafton Street, Dublin 2. Tel: 01-6056666 – see the opening page of the Bedroom section. Also at **Brown Thomas**), see John Rocha's perfectly clear Waterford Crystal lamps and a good selection of table lamps. Try **Lighting World** (James's Street, Dublin 8. Tel: 01-6717788) for art-deco-style wall lights. The homewares floor at **House of Fraser** (Dundrum Town Centre Dublin 14. Tel: 01-2991400) has a strong lighting section that's good for unusual table and standard lamps. Finding something in a traditional style can be hard. Vaughan Lighting is owned by an English couple who built up a collection of antique lamps

Top: ceiling light by Ensemble, available through **Milo Fitzgerald Interiors**.

Centre: musician Bobby MacMahon beside a standard lamp by Ensemble, typical of what you'll find at **Mobilia**.

Bottom: Louise Kennedy's chandelier for Tipperary Crystal, available at **Brown Thomas**.

and made copies of them. The lamps are sold through **Town & Country**. Prices go up to several hundred euro but start at about €50. The **Drawing Room** (Westbury Mall, Dublin 2. Tel: 01-6772083) is well known as a source for classic lamps – you'll always find something for a traditional interior. **Michael Connell Antiques** (54 Francis Street, Dublin 8. Tel: 01-4733898) is strong on light fittings, from desk lamps to lanterns.

High end

Consider lamps as sculpture. For something extraordinary and unique, **Niamh Barry** (Tel: 087-2319656; www.niamhbarrydesign.com) is a designer who custom-makes the kind of one-off feature light that helps give real character to a room. Barry does a lot of work for commercial clients (you can see her work at the Merrion Hotel and the Four Seasons). If you've got a double-height space and want something contemporary and exquisitely made, she's the person to contact. In Tom O'Rahilly's shop **Rua** (51 Lower George's Street, Dún Laoghaire, County Dublin. Tel: 01-2304209; www.rua.ie) you will find signature pieces with a refined ball base and drum shade. They cost from about €350 and will lift any space. The Santa & Cole standard lamp (pictured on pages 142 and 157) is one with which you can't go wrong. It is available in two sizes and costs from €510 at **Duff Tisdall** (Mill Street, Dublin 8. Tel: 01-4541355; and 537 North Circular Road, Dublin 1. Tel: 01-8558070). It has a tripod base and pleated linen shade. 'It's classic and isn't trying too hard. They've taken a standard lamp idea and made it quirky,' says architect Róisín Heneghan of Heneghan Peng, 'It traps the light in the pattern of the folds in the shade and would sit easily in a room with almost anything.' Achille Castiglioni designed the Toio lamp in 1962 and it is a brilliant design using basic mass-produced constituent parts – a fishing rod, car headlamp, transformer – which gives a beautiful light. It stands like a tall-stemmed flower – perfect for the corner of a room – and can be ordered through **Nordic Living** (57

Main Street, Blackrock, County Dublin. Tel: 01-2886680; www.nordicliving. ie). Another standard lamp I love is the Luxmaster lamp by Jasper Morrison (see page 168), which costs €400 at **Haus** (Crow Street and Pudding Row, Temple Bar, Dublin. Tel: 01-6795155; www.haus.ie). The stem is brushed steel and the lamp has a dimmer function. The cable wraps around the stem, exposing the functions, and it

casts a powerful light. See **Leo Scarff** for cool Irish-made lighting (www. leoscarffdesign.com), including lovely woven bentwood standard lamps from about €300 (See next page).

Sometimes you have to look abroad for lighting. Interior designer **Paul Austen** (Tel: 087-2360897) is agent for London-based Marianna Kennedy (see page 22 in the Living Room section). Her resin lamps can be ordered in

Left: art deco lamps from **Niall Mullen Antiques**, pictured at the home of John Lynch.

Centre: Garouste and Bonetti lighting, available through interior designer **Sirin Lewendon**.

Bottom: black lamp from **Haus**.

different colours and work in both
classical and contemporary settings.
She also does a standard lamp with
turned wood base and a shade made
from antique book cloth with gold leaf.
Prices for both on request.

We can't all gut our 19th-century
terraced house and pretend it's a
modern loft. Harsh minimalism is
being diluted, so experiment. Modern
lights look good in a traditional

setting and older lights look good in
modern apartments. A large chandelier
in a modern room makes a strong
statement. Louise Kennedy's two
chandeliers for Tipperary Crystal are
a great success: one is art deco style,
the other more traditional. Both can
be ordered at **Brown Thomas** and
provide instant razzle-dazzle. **Clancy
Chandeliers** (Ballywaltrim. Bray,
County Wicklow. Tel: 01-2863460) is

the place to find beautiful chandeliers: some prices are high but you can also get something nice for €1500. **Bygone Days** (The Cottage, Killashee House Hotel, Naas, County Kildare. Tel: 045-901251; www.bygonedays. com) also does pretty chandeliers in various sizes. **SKI Interiors** has a range of traditional crystal chandeliers available to order. **Duff Tisdall** has a modern version of a shaded chandelier and also a good lighting section in general, particularly table lamps. Also see **www.architecturalclassics.com** for antique lighting and chandeliers. Tess and Galen Bales of **Warehouse 39** are suppliers for Venetia Studium lights from Venice (www.venetiastudium. com; contact info@w39.ie for country-wide stockists). The silk shades on standard lamps and ceiling lights have intricate patterns hand-painted by Italian craftsmen (see the opening page of the Living Room section for picture). Stylewise they're part Moroccan, part old Italian. Prices start at about €2000. Another Warehouse 39 specialist lighting range from Italy is Melograno Blu (www.melogranoblu.com). Shades are crafted from mouth-blown glass to form spectacular pendants, lamps and chandeliers that are breathtaking one-off pieces.

Also try: **Lamps & Lighting** (1 Terenure Road, Rathgar, Dublin 6. Tel: 01-49101850); **Bob Bushell** (Sir John Rogerson's Quay, Dublin 2. Tel: 01 671-0044; www.bobbushell. com); **Bective Lights** (70 St Laurence's Park, Stillorgan, County Dublin. Tel: 01-2831151); **Erco Lighting** (289 Harold's Cross Road,Dublin 6w Tel: 01-4966177); **Lightworks** (North Link Industrial Estate, Dundalk, County Louth. Tel: 042-9356014); **Light Plan** (Penrose House, Penrose Quay, Cork. Tel: 021-4500665 and Richmond Road, Dublin 3. Tel: 01-8360200).

HANGING PICTURES

Good art can have an amazing effect on a room. Live with what you love – that's what counts. My favourite gallery is the **Cross** (59 Francis Street Tel: 01-4738978): they always have a stock of beautiful works.

Make sure you frame and hang art

Far right top: fashion stylist Catherine Condell's 'wall of fame'.

Centre: Maria MacVeigh's living room with Gary Coyle print.

Bottom: a picture shelf from **Inreda** on Camden Street.

Near right top: 1940s poster from **Gallery 29** on Molesworth Street.

Bottom: fashion stylist Graham Cruz's collection of religious iconography, hung with attitude.

correctly. Gallery owner Ib Jorgensen uses framer **Liam Slattery** (Tel: 01-4978446) in Rathmines. Slattery works at the top end of the market and his framing is particularly beautiful, if expensive. Event designer Tara Fay, on the other hand, uses **Framemakers** in Stillorgan Industrial Estate, Blackrock, County Dublin (Tel: 01-2954500), a company that caters to various budgets but still does a good job.

A person to note is **Jane Williams** (Tel: 087-7819965), who learnt to gild through various apprenticeships, first at the studio of Emily Napier at Loughcrew and then in New York at Sothebys, where she gilded blackamoors for Joan Collins. Jane started her own studio in Portobello a while ago and examples of her work in public spaces include the ceiling of Dublin's City Hall and the gates and railings of Powerscourt House in Wicklow. She will restore furniture, picture frames, portrait frames and overmantel mirrors.

Art collections are usually built up gradually over a number of years but if you have the opportunity to hang a

group of paintings at one time (after repainting a room, for example) lay them out on the floor and move them around until you find a good visual balance. If they differ greatly in size use the biggest as your starting point. A large painting has a big influence on how a room is going to look and there are probably only a few places it can hang. Keep big bold images high and detailed ones lower so they can be seen easily. Consider how paintings look against one another. It might help to create imaginary lines on the wall – a horizontal line with pictures arranged above and below, or a few vertical lines that make centre points for the column arrangements. Keep the same amount of space between each two picture frames. Juxtapose horizontal and vertical paintings in a small group.

A picture shelf lends casual style to a room and allows you to rearrange photographs and paintings without destroying walls with picture hooks. **Inreda** (71 Lower Camden Street, Dublin 8. Tel: 01-4760362; www. inreda.ie) sells a 160-cm shelf with

a low ridge to hold the pictures in place for €115, and a 180-cm version for €135. Both are made from oak, which you could make unobtrusive by painting the same colour as your walls.

Having a painting or drawing framed professionally is always a better option but if you must, **Habitat** (6-10 Suffolk Street, Dublin 2. Tel: 01-6771433; Fairgreen Road, Galway. Tel: 091-569980; and 41 Arthur Street, Belfast BT1 4GB. Tel: 028-90249522) is the best for basic ready-made frames.

TK Maxx (branches countrywide) always has a good selection of small photograph frames: it's hard to spend more than €10. **Brown Thomas** has a good mix of mirrored, wood and lacquered frames.

WALL OF FAME

'Because of the work I do, I get to meet a lot of people,' says stylist Catherine Condell. The wall inside the front door of her Dublin home is hung with photographs (see previous page). You could do something similar. Although there are notes from Daniel Day Lewis and John Malkovich, the majority of photographs are of friends. There are drawings, too, including a sketch by designer Mariad Whisker of a dress she made for Condell to wear to a wedding.

Left: a wood fireplace from **Kilkenny Architectural Salvage & Antiques**.

Right: a stove from **Fenton Fires**.

'I like pictures propped: you don't always have to hang them.' The photographic piece pictured on the previous page is by Gary Coyle (available at the **Kevin Kavanagh Gallery**, 66 Great Strand St, Dublin 1. Tel: 01-8740064).

Alternatively, choose something bright and cheering: Anne and John Rogers of **Gallery 29 (**29 Molesworth Street, Dublin 2. Tel: 01-6425784) met while studying art history in Savannah, Georgia. She is from the US, he is Irish, and they opened a gallery to sell vintage posters. Rogers is 'addicted to French movie posters' but also sells travel, film, music, tobacco and alcohol images. Prices range from €40 to €4000 but most posters cost €300-€400.

FIREPLACES

It's good to make the hearth quite large and deep in a small room; it adds to the feeling of space.

At **Kilkenny Architectural Salvage & Antiques** (Tel: 056-7764434) you will find lovely wood fireplace surrounds that don't cost a lot: for example, the one pictured opposite left, at a house in Blackrock cost just €120.

Hearth & Home (Fonthill Retail Park, Dublin 22. Tel: 01-6200100 www.hearthandhome.ie) is particularly good for modern gas fires: see the Modern Architectural and Bonart & Gonay ranges first. **Fenton Fires** (Church Road, Greystones, County Wicklow. Tel: 01-2874310) is worth a look, especially for stoves, as is **Kilkenny Living** (Ballyhale, County Kilkenny. Tel: 056-7766796). **Belle Cheminée** (106 Capel Street, Dublin 1. Tel: 01-8724122) sells both contemporary and traditional chimneypieces in all sorts of stones and marbles – some simple, some ornate. Ask about the Bolection sandstone fireplaces. **Artefaction** (12-13 Lime Street, Dublin 2. Tel: 01-6776495; www.artefaction.ie) does large-scale antique-looking carved marble chimneypieces as well as simple elegant modern versions in a variety of stones.

STORAGE

BOOKSHELVES

Books are like old friends. They add texture and personality to your life and you want to know where they are when you need them. If you have lots of books, you must have a place to put them, and bookshelves are great organisers for anywhere in the house – not only for books but for other objects. Whether you purchase a bookcase or have it made by a cabinetmaker, always plan on more shelves than you think you need. Books have a way of multiplying.

Vitsoe shelving starts at €100 per shelf at **mimo design** (Fountainstown, County Cork. Tel: 021-4833443; www. mimodesign.ie). It's a modular system and the cost depends on what size you need. It can be bought in all sorts of configurations and mimo will give a quote over the phone. You can add more as finances allow: this is long-term stuff, designed by Dieter Rams in 1960 and produced continuously ever since. Made from metal, it

can be wall mounted and is very sturdy. Visually, it provides a neutral structure for whatever you display. For inexpensive modern ready-mades try **Habitat**'s Matrix system: €85 for a 20-shelf unit. At **Mobilia** ask about shelving by Casamania: for around €300 you will get a 1.5m-high and 1m-long bookcase. At **Mimosa Interiors** (Dún Laoghaire Shopping Centre. Tel: 01-2808166 and Cranford Centre, Stillorgan Road, Dublin 4. Tel: 01-2602443) you will find great 8-ft-high painted bookcases from €3000: what's nice about them is that they look like the real thing – a faded heirloom – not a brand-new reproduction. **Argos** (branches countrwide) isn't glamorous or cool but its catalogue sometimes offers a good buy. Their single shelves in beech or walnut effect cost €24.99. They can be used anywhere in the home – bathroom, kitchen or living room. They have a decent depth so they can hold a variety of objects, and would be good for books or decorative items. They float on the wall, thanks to invisible fixings.

Get inspired. A book to add to your new shelves should be *Modern Glamour: The Art of Unexpected Style* by Kelly Wearstler. Also peruse any book about the 1960s decorator David Hicks. For more inspiration, rent *Pillow Talk*, in which Doris Day plays an interior designer, and Hitchcock's *North by Northwest*, which features a fantastic Frank Lloyd Wright-type house. The upbeat Hollywood style will cheer you up.

CUSTOM-MADE UNITS

Have a carpenter make bookshelves or cupboards. It's all about finding someone who'll do the job well but not over-charge. In Cork, try **Noel Barry Joinery** (Tel: 021-4652844) to make storage units. Dublin-based interior designer Deirdre Whelan used joiners at **Period Design** in Cavan (Tel: 049-9522323) to make low MDF shelving units for her home. Michela Mantero, another designer, uses **Natural Wood Designs,** Rathmiles, Killenard, Portarlington, County Laois (Tel: 057-8626483; 087-2761684) to make fitted units. I've also heard good things about **Tony Harkin** (Tel: 087-2227372), who is more a furniture designer than anything else: go to him for

From left: oak-and-iron shelving from the **Enniskerry Trading Company**; a rattan magazine bin from **House of Ireland**; a mirrored chest by Knowles & Christou from **Studio44**; a patterned glass cabinet from the same company; a cabinet from **Eminence**.

something imaginative. **Alan Gallagher** (Tel: 087-2265362) is another good cabinetmaker, as is Therese Martin of **Martin Design** (Tel: 086-2528166). You could also try **Oakline** (8 Ranelagh, Dublin 6. Tel: 01-4977435: Unit 1, Greenhills Business Park, Tallaght, Dublin 24. Tel: 01-4626676; www.oakline.ie), which offers good craftsmanship. This company makes kitchens, bedroom furniture, bookcases and office furniture. From a studio in west Cork, **Eric Pearce**'s (Tel: 023-49852; epearce@eircom.net) reputation for special commissions has spread to the UK, where he works closely with several interior designers.

For Jasper Conran's apartment he built a tall oak drinks cabinet with antique glass panels. Public commissions have included oak tables for the dining hall in Trinity College and suites of furniture for the Taoiseach's department in Government Buildings in Dublin. Private commissions are part of an overall interior design service.

BOXES AND BASKETS

Hide that mess. It'll make you feel much better. Don't leave **House of Ireland** (37 Nassau Street, Dublin 2. Tel: 01-6711111). without a giant rattan magazine bin. Prices start at about €150. It's sturdy and will

have a transforming effect. Put it next to your sofa or behind it – and just tidy away those magazines. Kathleen McCormack's shop, **Basket Barn** (Watering Hollow, Ballinkill, Broadford, County Kildare. Tel: 086-8807208; www.basketbarn.ie) stocks an array of log baskets, kitchen-drawer baskets, herb baskets and flower baskets. They look great even in the most contemporary interior. I love her lidded trunk baskets that could be used for linen, toys or any number of things.

Next (Dundrum Town Centre, Dublin 14 and branches countrywide. Tel: 01-2051310) usually has birch trunks with drawers inside for magazines and CDs.

Blinding fluorescent light doesn't make **TK Maxx** a pleasant place to shop but you'll pick up good baskets and storage boxes very cheaply. The Blanchardstown branch is better than the Stephen's Green Centre in Dublin.

CHESTS OF DRAWERS

Mobilia has furniture that takes inspiration from high-end stuff but at a more affordable price. It is particularly good for chests that could be used in a bedroom, living room or dining room: think modern. **Bob Bushell** is always worth a look for contemporary storage. At **Inreda** seek out the snow cabinet

– it comes in all sorts of configurations and prices start at €500. For something traditional in light timbers such as beech and oak, Irish company **Molloy Wood Crafts** (Scariff Road, Whitegate, County Clare. Tel: 061-926000; www.molloywoodcrafts.ie) make solid chests and other freestanding units. The Milan range is best: a vaguely Shaker style with tongue-and-groove side panelling. All pieces are sanded for a natural aged look. **Fired Earth** has chests and shelving made from reclaimed teak: most have a colonial style. Meanwhile, **Serendipity** (70 Rathgar Avenue, Dublin 6. Tel: 01-4925572) sells painted chests and dressers from about €500. **Mac's Salvage Warehouse** (749 South Circular Road, Islandbridge, Dublin 8. Tel: 01-6792110) is a treasure trove for cheap old everything – chests, sideboards, bookcases – in traditional styles.

CABINETS

Knowles & Christou, an English company distributed in Ireland through **www.studio44.ie**, makes the beautiful patterned glass cabinet on tapered legs pictured on the previous page. It's called LuLu and costs €5650. The doors and sides are printed glass. Inside, there are glass shelves and a lacquered paper interior. At **Fassbinder & English** (Old Fire Station, George's Place, Dún Laoghaire. County Dublin. Tel: 01-2360683; www.fassbinderenglish.com) custom-makes cabinets that could be used for books, display or as a linen press. For example, a cabinet with a glass-panelled door, antique ivory finish and aged gilding costs €4500. The style of this piece is French but the company has a wide repertoire and specialises in unusual surface finishes. Within reason, they can work to a budget on a particular piece. **Limited Edition** (96 Francis Street, Dublin 8. Tel: 01-4531123) has 1930s-style sycamore cabinets with sliding doors (for €4900) that can be ordered in various stains and could be used for storing almost anything: the shelves are just the right height for standard hardbacks. As mentioned already, you could always have something made by a furniture designer: Laura Mays (**Yaffe Mays Furniture**, Salruck, Renvyle,

County Galway. Tel: 095-43089; www. lauramays.com) trained as an architect and now makes all sorts of furniture, including cabinets with pull-out drawers fronted in different woods and with leather loop handles. She also makes bookcases and display units. **Flanagans Of Buncrana** (Deerpark Road, Mount Merrion.Tel: 01-2880218) can be worth a look for freestanding cabinets, bookcases and other units, usually in a mock repro style. **Instore** (Limerick, Tel: 061-416088; Waterford, Tel: 051-844882; Galway, Tel: 091-530085 and Sligo, Tel: 071-9149174) is good for white units with low presses and glass-panelled doors for €399 or big chests of drawers for €499.

SHOPPING IN BELFAST

Begin your Belfast shopping trip on the Lisburn Road. This long avenue, with its quirky, varied shops, is a great place to explore. Start at **Beaufort Interiors** (597 Lisburn Rd. Tel: 028-90664655), which is roughly half-way down the road. Beaufort decorate the homes of affluent Belfast and have some expensive things such as a Fendi dining table for £7000. Matching chairs? They are £1600 each. But not everything is as dear and the showroom is big, with plenty of relaxed style. Good buys include two 1950s-style bent plywood chairs with green tweed panels, costing £300. Beaufort may have great brands – Flos, Poliform, Missoni, and Porada

Left: A customer at **Beaufort Interiors**.

Right: Suzanne Garuda of **Garuda Design.**

– but look specifically for stand-out pieces, in particular, pricey but wonderful fabrics (£150 per metre) and wallpapers (from £60 per roll).

Near Beaufort is a cute shop called **An Angel at My Table** (537 Lisburn Rd; Tel: 028-90681100). There is plenty of the painted French-Swedish look in pale grey. More interesting are their mirrored 1930s-style dressing tables and red lacquered armchairs. You could also pick up some tableware here. Then there is is a tiny shop called **Kitty Galore** (577 Lisburn Rd. Tel: 028-90681118), which has great retro vases and china. Next, go to the Boucher Road area. It's essentially one big retail park, but the shop to visit is **Dekko** (52 Boucher Road. Tel: 028-90508600; www.shopdekko.com). What they sell resembles a cheaper version of Habitat, but there's a flat-pack look to a lot of the furniture, so be careful. Look for basics. I love the Tasia dining chair in powder-blue (£39) and the small-kitchen-sized Zoom table (£135).

Afterwards, walk across the road to **Au Natural** (Abbey Trading Centre, Longwood Road, Newtownabbey.

Tel: 028-90869470), a discount shop with lots of mirrors, vases, baskets and bathroom bits and pieces.

Make your way to the city centre and visit **Equinox** (32 Howard St, Belfast BT1 6PF. Tel: 028-90230089) and **Still** (Royston House, Upper Queen Street. Tel: 028-90466088). You can walk from one to the other in a few minutes. Equinox stocks lots of small items such as glassware (Alvar Aalto vases), tableware (Alessi) and bedlinen (Armani Casa). **Still** has contemporary furniture, which can be delivered anywhere in the country. Quality is good and prices reasonable. Don't bother with the sofas, which are nothing special – instead look at things like a neat slat-front freestanding wardrobe (£600) or low curved coffee table (£300).

Two other shops that should be visited together are **Garuda Design** (Maxol Building, 261-3 Ormeau Road. Tel: 028-90692626; www. garudadesign.com) and the **Yard** (Montgomery Road. Tel: 028-90405600; www.theyard.co.uk). Interior designer Suzanne Garuda is the

sister of Dublin-based designer Sirin Lewendon and her shop is strong on statement pieces. It has atmosphere with a definite 'look' that's rich but not cloying and that mixes lots of styles. Colours are often beige, black, gold, silver. The Yard is a little off the beaten track at the end of a laneway in an industrial park, but it's renowned for stocking the best bathroom fittings in the North.

GIFTS

Chef Lu Thornely suggests gift ideas for foodies: 'Pia Bang ((Pia Bang Home, South Anne Street, Dublin 2. Tel: 01-8883777) usually has lovely glass or ceramic cake stands, all very pretty and reasonably priced from about €15. At Kitchen Complements (Chatham St, Dublin 2.

Tel: 01 6770734) a sophisticated potato masher costs €32.75. It's something most people don't have, but it is the way to get restaurant-style creamy mash, and it can also be used for turnips, parsnips and other root vegetables – just put everything in and twist.'

Below are ideas for finding a home-related gift. I'm talking about small gifts, not big meaningful statements.

Louise Kennedy's inimitable style fills the house (56 Merrion Square, Dublin 2) that acts as her showroom, shop and home. On the ground floor is a room given over to the most perfect gifts in town: desktop items by David Linley, the full range of glass Louise designs for Tipperary Crystal, unusual French and Italian perfumes for men and women, pretty little silver items, super-refined silk faux flowers…

From left: a cake stand from **Pia Bang Home**; a porcelain tea-light holder from **the Narrow Space Gallery** in Clonmel (www. thenarrowspacecom); **Louise Kennedy**, 56 Merrion Square, Dublin 2.

Top: a candle from
Brown Thomas

Bottom: give a lemon tree
from **Mackeys Garden
Centre,** Castlepark Road,
Sandycove, County
Dublin: Tel: 01-2807385.
They cost about €70.

everything is high on luxury. Plus the wrapping is smart. Upstairs is another room with more of the same, but also men's shirts to her design, cashmere throws, cute kids clothes by Triple Star, and so on. Not many think of it but this is one of the best little shops in Dublin if you are looking for a present.

No 6 is Helen McAlinden's fashion and interiors shop (6 Castle Market, Dublin 2. Tel: 01-6723904). Apart from her clothing, she sells furniture (great glass lamps and big distressed metal mirrors) but what you'll find in terms of gifts are Foxford bedlinen, towels and throws. McAlinden designs these products, giving a fresh twist to their great quality. See also Foxford candles and room scent. Within the range you'll find something for everyone: soft greys for minimalists; blue checks for traditionalists.

Waterford Crystal mightn't seem like the most original gift but it's still one of the most welcome. Why? Because it's beautiful, expensive and not really the kind of thing you'd buy for yourself. I like John Rocha's opulent black glass range, not so much for the glassware

but for the vases and bowls, which start at about €200 at **Brown Thomas.** The new clear-glass range is great too, lighter than before and with a band of cut pattern. Waterford is always welcome as a gift for young people or as a house-warming. Take a look at the cute black tea-light holders for €45. Even one makes a sweet present.

Muji (5 Chatham St, Dublin 2. Tel: 01-6794591) is a good shop to pick something up for those who like modern design. Also go there for men in general: they have great gadgety things such as radios for the shower and miniature cardboard stereo speakers. Stay well away from their clothing, which tends to be utilitarian, and choose nice bathroom goods and kitchenware. Something might look terribly plain and unexciting to you but your design-head friend will love it.

At the other extreme is **Avoca** (11-13 Suffolk Street, Dublin 2 Tel: 01-6774215, Kilmacanogue, County Wicklow. Tel: 01- 2864476, and branches countrywide: see www. avoca.ie for details). This is for those who like homey bits with plenty of character and fun. Director Amanda Pratt is a lifestyle genius and you'll always find a gift suitable for your sister or aunt. Quirky bathroom bits and colourful kitchen stuff such as delph and glassware are perfect. What I like best are the Avoca wool and mohair throws in zingy colours that cost about €45.

Brown Thomas has buckets of gift-type items on the third floor but I love their selection of candles. Look at True Grace, Diptique and Kenneth Turner: my favourite is downstairs in the perfume area – the Comme des Garçons 2 candle has a whiff of incense but isn't too church-like. Also in Brown Thomas, you can't go wrong with really good bedlinen from Bottom Drawer. Anything by Magimix makes a good gift – juicers and ice-cream makers are sold on the third floor.

Belle Maison (57a Glasthule Road, Dún Laoghaire, County Dublin. Tel: 01-2303083) is a cute little shop packed with cute things that don't cost a lot and make handy gifts. Imagine old-fashioned wall clocks, dainty china, padded hangers and smart aprons. While in the area, visit **Formality** (The Cowshed, Glasthule Village, County Dublin. Tel: 01-2808071). You'll find cool gifts for gardening friends.

Stock sells furniture but also smaller items that make good gifts. For example, there are colourful doormats with stripes or sunflowers; unusual kitchen things such as salad-dressing makers; and coloured glasses and jugs by LSA (black, electric-blue, harp-green). Incidentally, they also have some of the best folding chairs around for about €90.

Six Times Tables (www.sixtimestables. com) isn't a shop but a collective of six of the best craft designers in the country. For example, one of Michèle Hannan's hand-built clay vessels could stand alone but they're designed to relate to each other as a pair, with organic shapes that interlock. What all this means for your table is a sculptural object that will add height in the centre, (the tallest of the vessels is half-a-metre high), not to mind a bit of interest and a readymade conversation-starter. The vessels cost between €140 and €360.

Patrick G. Hall, on the other hand, took inspiration from traditional china

Top: soaps from **Muji**.

Bottom: a vase by Louise Kennedy for Tipperary Crystal.

183

Top: John Rocha
at **Debenhams**.

Centre: right: doll's house
from **Brown Thomas**.

Bottom: decorations
from **Brown Thomas**.

patterns for dinner plates, but gave them a modern edge by enlarging the pattern in a wide border, which is textured using a technique that involves rolling lace into wet clay. There are various serving dishes in the range, priced from €30. The largest plate is slightly sunken and could be used to float candles.

Another Six Times Tables craftsperson is Liz Nilsson, a textile artist who has produced tabletop pieces that are screen-printed on heavy linen. Runners cost €75 and napkins €15 each. The runners might appeal to those who want to show the wood of a table rather than cover it with a tablecloth. Liz suggests that runners can also be placed over a plain tablecloth to add colour and texture.

Also try: **Robert Lee's Japanese Ceramics**, (Durrus Road, Ballydehob, County Cork. Tel: 087-1271903; www.robertleeceramics.com) for fluid, elegant, black and jade-green vases; the **Monogram Shop** (Tel: 01-236 0311; www.monogram.ie) for personalised bedlinen, towels or anything fabric-based; **Granny's Bottom Drawer** (53

Main Street Kinsale, County Cork. Tel: 021-4773616) for linen sheets; **Inside Out** (97 Lower George's Street, Dún Laoghaire, County Dublin. Tel: 01-2148685) for garden things; **House of Ireland** (37 Nassau Street, Dublin 2. Tel: 01-6711111) is clearly aimed at tourists but don't overlook it for gift possibilities – go straight to the back of the shop for tableware and glass.

CHRISTMAS:
A FEW IDEAS

The **Chester Beatty Library Gift Shop**, Dublin Castle, Dublin 2 (Tel: 01-4070750). If you want an exotic, non-traditional tree, every year the museum has papier mâché decorations from the north of India; fairies from South Africa and Thailand and hand-carved wood figures from Italy and Russia. They cost from €13.95 and are festive but not in the usual red-and-green way.

The **Drawing Room,** Westbury Mall, Dublin 2 (Tel: 01-6772083). For a Christmas tree decorated as a jewel, this shop always has a bit of sparkle, such as clear glass beads in crystal and dangling diamond drops. For the mantel, you'll find small wire trees covered in glass beads – use two or three together.

Dunnes Home (South Great George's Street, Dublin 2, Cornelscourt, Dublin 18, and large Dunnes Stores branches countrywide). This is the place for inexpensive tableware. Get extra glasses and china here if you're catering for large numbers.

Pia Bang Home (2 South Anne Street, Dublin 2. Tel: 01-8883777). Each Christmas Bang's shop has the cutest decorations, with a touch of Scandinavia: painted wooden toys such as fire engines and aeroplanes or elves and Santas made from canvas. At Christmas the whole shop is beautifully done in traditional style, full of charming, covetable objects.

The **Pen Corner** (12 College Green, Dublin 2. Tel: 01-6793641). This may not be the first place you'd think of for decorations but they have a stash of festive, dressed-up dolls in 1950s eveningwear for about €10. They could be used almost anywhere for humorous effect. Some have gold wings; others sit

Clockwise from top left: timber mirror from the **Enniskerry Trading Company**; singer Camille O'Sullivan at her art deco dressing table. Find something similar at **www.the antiquewarehouse. com**; a wall-mounted dresser at the home of chef Lu Thornely – an auction-room find.

on a cloud and play music. Kitsch, yes – but in a good way.

Jungle Flowers, Malahide and Rush (Tel: 01-8454633), do some of the best wreaths around. Some are artificial; others are made from real flowers – they will deliver both. Also see their annual dancing-girl tree decorations.

Eve Home Accessories (Meridian Point, Greystones, County Wicklow. Tel: 01-2016358) have little reindeer made from dried leaves (€35) and snowmen made from cardboard with fur around the neck (€13.50). Large wreaths made from twigs (€65) could be used inside as well as out.

Save time and effort by having someone else do your pre-Christmas cleaning blitz. There are many cleaning companies but three that I recommend are: **Southside Contract and Carpet Cleaners** (Tel: 01-8879006); **Hibernian Cleaning** (Tel: 01-4780433; 01-4783000); and **Octopus Cleaning** (Tel: 086-8312957). Southside and Hibernian are large-scale cleaners but employ good staff and are thorough and fast. Octopus, on the other hand, are a husband-and-wife team who will

spend a day doing a complete blitz – washing windows, cleaning the cooker, polishing fireplaces and so on.

Have carpets and sofas protected against spillages. **Fiber Seal** (1-800-789100) will treat against spills and stains such as red wine. Prices start at about €200 for a carpet and the service is offered countrywide.

Before decorations and other Christmas paraphernalia hit the house, get rid of as much junk as possible – rooms will look bigger and brighter. **Ros Sparks** (Tel: 086-8137984) offers a decluttering service and, as a mother of three, organisation is her forte. She will tackle your attic, garage, under-stairs storage, kitchen or the whole house. An hour-long briefing occurs the day before decluttering, then a skip arrives and Ros divides everything into piles to keep, dump, give to charity and recycle. The process takes a day, at the end of which Ros removes the bundles. She's discreet too. 'No one wants anyone to know they're doing this – some wives don't even tell their husbands.'

INTERIORITY COMPLEX

Orna Mulcahy

My neighbour felt the time had come to do something about her living room carpet. It was perfectly good, she said, a little worn in places, but she'd never been entirely happy with the colour, a dense bottle-green. Eventually, she had it pulled up – the underlay had worn away to dust – and the new carpet arrived in all its pale-mushroom splendour. Still, she was sorry to see the old carpet go, having lived with it since 1962.

'Forty-three years!' the carpet fitter spluttered. 'Sure these days people change their carpet every three years.'

My neighbour was horrified but she loves her new carpet and the way it makes her previously rather dreary living room look so peaceful and welcoming. Only thing is, now the curtains are letting it down. That's the trouble with decorating: once you start, it's very hard to stop. When is a room ever really finished to perfection, and if you do get it just right, does that make you want to start all over again to create an entirely new look?

Having gone for the complete French armchair and armoire look, complete with toile scatter-cushions, are you now ready to chuck it out and introduce the low-slung Italian corner sofa and sleek walnut sideboard?

Are you bored with the relentlessly cool limestone-effect bathroom tiles and yearning for some nice shimmery mosaic? Is that freestanding basin annoying you and would you prefer something timeless from Armitage Shanks? Has the built-in stainless-steel-finish cappuccino machine ever actually worked, or do you really prefer tea?

While the decoration and enjoyment of our homes has become ever more important to us as the economy booms and people's standards soar, we're also learning that home improvement can be a continuous process, rather than a project with a beginning, middle and end.

Fuelled by glossy interiors magazines and makeover programmes on TV, not to mention the property supplement full of gorgeous houses, we're on a constant renovation roll, made possible by reasonably priced homewares through warehouse-style outlets, and a new interior design boutique on every corner.

As one interior designer puts it, 'At every stage now, people are refining and embellishing and enjoying the final results.'

That's a daunting thought for beginners, who want to create a stylish home but are unsure how to go about it. Even with the right shade of paint, the right shape of sofa and the appropriate number of rolled-up towels and scented pebbles in the bathroom, there needs to be something more to make a home look and feel right. Slowly we are coming around to the idea that individuality is important. The best interiors are idiosyncratic.

They cannot be bought off the peg. They cannot be copied exactly from a magazine. Instead they have to be built up stage by stage and layer by layer. That means making changes by degrees, learning from mistakes and not being in too much of a hurry.

The famous American decorator Nancy Lancaster, who was credited with creating the country-house look in postwar England, mixed the most unlikely items – expensive needlepoint cushions on an old armchair upholstered in a dyed damask table cloth.

Fully renovated houses are beginning to look the same. There's an inevitability about the pale-painted walls, the wall-to-wall pale timbers, the granite-topped kitchens, the atriums, the plasma screen over the fireplace, the fully decked garden.

Now perhaps it's time for people to let their homes relax a little and evolve.

Which means that the next big thing could be clutter.

Orna Mulcahy is Property Editor of The Irish Times.

SUPPLIERS' CONTACT DETAILS

20th-Century Furniture at **Habitat**, 6-10 Suffolk Street, Dublin 2. Tel: 01-6770679.
Adams, Blackrock, Co. Dublin. Tel: 01-2865146.
Allabri, The Mall, Riverside Way, Midleton, Co. Cork. Tel: 021-4634131.
Alliance Property Maintenance, Unit Q6, Greenogue Business Park, Rathcoole, Co. Dublin. Tel: 01-4013970.
Amelia Aran, 71 York Road, Dún Laoghaire, Co. Dublin. Tel: 01-2805877; www.ameliaaran.com.
An Angel at My Table, 537 Lisburn Rd Belfast BT9 7GQ; Tel: 028-90681100.
O'Connor, Angela, 9 Leopardstown Avenue, Blackrock, Co. Dublin. Tel: 01-2888811.
Antica, Earlscourt Industrial Estate, Beaumount Avenue, Churchtown, Dublin 14. Tel: 01-2960136; www.antica.ie.
Antique Warehouse, www.theantiquewarehouse.ie.
Antiques Fairs Ireland. Tel: 087-2670607; www.antiquesfairsireland.com.
Arena Kitchen & Bathrooms, 3-4 Cardiff Lane, Sir John Rogerson's Quay, Dublin 2. Tel: 01-6715365.
Argos (countrywide).
Arnotts, Henry Street, Dublin 1. Tel: 01-8050400.
Around the Irish House, Dromiskin, Co. Louth. Tel: 042-9382890.
Arroo, Co. Leitrim. Tel: 071-9856997; www.arroo.ie.
Artefaction, 12-13 Lime Street, Dublin 2. Tel: 01-6776495.
Ashgrove Interiors, Ballybrittas, Co. Laois. Tel: 057-8626290.
Asian Silk Road, Unit 95, Malahide Road Industrial Park, Dublin 17. Tel: 01-8485044.
At Home with Clery's, Unit 2, Leopardstown Retail Park, Dublin 18. Tel: 01-2941710.
Au Natural, Abbey Trading Centre, Longwood Rd, Newtownabbey BT37 9UQ. Tel: 028-90869470.
AuroKlee Paper, 89 North Circular Road, Dublin 7. Tel: 01-8383544.
Aurora Lighting Design & Supply. Tel: 01-4549837.
Austen, Paul. Tel: 087-2391757.
Avoca, 11-13 Suffolk Street, Dublin 2. Tel: 01-6774215, Kilmacanogue, Co. Wicklow. Tel: 01- 2864476, and branches countrywide: www.avoca.ie.

B&Q (countrywide).
Baggot Framing Gallery, 13 Eastmoreland Place, Dublin 4. Tel: 01-6606063.
Bain, David. Tel: 087-2584190.
Barry, Niamh. Tel: **087-2319656;** www.niamhbarrydesign.com.
Basket Barn, Watering Hollow, Ballinkill, Broadford, Co. Kildare. Tel: 086-8807208; www.basketbarn.ie.
Beaufort Interiors, 597 Lisburn Rd, Belfast BT9 7GS. Tel: 028-90664655.
Bective Lights, 70 Street. Laurence's Park, Stillorgan, Co. Dublin. Tel: 01-2831151.
Bedroom Studio, The, 26 Castle Street, Dalkey, Co. Dublin. Tel: 01-235 2815; www.bedroomstudio.ie.
Bell, Michael, Vicarstown, Co. Laois. Tel:

057-8625633 www.michaelbelldesign.com.
Belle Maison, 57A Glasthule Road, Dún Laoghaire, Co. Dublin. Tel: 01-2303083.
Bellissima, Distillery Road, Bandon, Co. Cork. Tel: 023-54740; www.bellissima.ie.
Benedicts, Avondale Hall, Carysfort Avenue, Blackrock, Co. Dublin. Tel: 01-2881693.
BL. Curtains Direct. Tel: 061-355974/ 087-2058514.
Blue Door, The, 21 Poplar Avenue, Naas Town Centre, Co. Kildare. Tel: 045-901573.
Bob Bushell, Sir John Rogerson's Quay, Dublin 2. Tel: 01 671-0044; www.bobbushell.com.
Brennan, Lorraine, Fifty-Eight B, 10 North Great George's Street, Dublin 1. Tel: 01-8735420, www.fiftyeightb.ie.
Brian S. Nolan, 102 Upper George's Street, Dún Laoghaire. Tel: 01-2800564.
Brown Thomas, Grafton Street, Dublin 2. Tel: 01-6056666.
BTW, www.btw.ie.
Buckley, Philippa, www.studio44.ie.
Buckleys, Sandycove, Co. Dublin Tel: 01-2300193.
Buggy, Margaret, Tel: 059-9159981.
Bushfield Interiors, Dunleer, Co. Louth. Tel: 041-685 1028.
Bygone Days, The Cottage, Killashee, Naas, Co. Kildare. Tel: 045-901251.

Carter, Orla. Tel: 01-2980371.
Casa, Blackrock, Co. Dublin. Tel: 01-2805805.
Casey's Furniture, 65 Oliver Plunkett Street, Cork. Tel: 021-4270393; and Raheen, Limerick. Tel: 061-307070.
Cash & Carry Kitchens. Nine showrooms in Dublin, Cork, Limerick and Galway; see www.cashandcarrykitchens.com.
Castle Curtains & Blinds, 1a Three Rock Road, Sandyford Industrial Estate, Co. Dublin. Tel: 01-2955100.
Ceadogan Rugs, Wellington Bridge, Co. Wexford. Tel: 051-561349.
Chalon (6 Main Street, Blackrock, County Dublin. Tel: 01-2835525).
Chester Beatty Library Gift Shop, Dublin Castle, Dublin 2. Tel: 01-4070750.
Christy Bird, 32 Richmond Street South, Dublin 2. Tel: 01-4750409.
Clancy Chandeliers, Ballywaltrim. Bray, Co. Wicklow. Tel: 01-2863460.
Classic Floors, Unit B4, KCR Industrial Estate, Dublin 12. Tel: 01-4924944.
Classic Furniture, The Park, Carrickmines, Co. Dublin. Tel: 01-2076566; for other branches see www.classicfurniture.ie.
Clerys, O'Connell Street, Dublin. Tel: 01-8786000.
Clever Clogs, www.cleverclogs.ie) **Coach House Kitchens**, Carhue, Coachford, Co. Cork. Tel: 021-7334098; www.coach-house-kitchens.com
Collection, The, Unit 4, Street Helen's Court, Lower George's Street, Dún Laoghaire, Co. Dublin. Tel: 01-2147700; www.the-collection.ie.
Collins, Orla, www.purple-design.com.
Costello Flowers, Northumberland Avenue, Dún Laoghaire, Co. Dublin. Tel:

01-2841864.
Country Interiors, Abbey Street, Cahir, Co. Tipperary. Tel: 052-41187 www.frenchcountryinteriors.ie.
Cremins Moiselle, the Design Centre, Bray South Business Park, Killarney Road, Bray, Co. Wicklow. Tel: 01-204 2848; www.creminsmoiselle.com.
Cross Gallery, The, 59 Francis Street, Dublin 8, Tel: 01-4738978.
Cruise, Sarah, e-mail: sarah@designintervention.ie.
Crystal & Silk, 1 Michael Street, Wexford. Tel: 053-9144203.
Curtain and Gift Traders, The, Newtown Park Avenue, Blackrock, Co. Dublin. Tel: 01-2836547.
Curtain Exchange, Adelaide Court, Albert Road, Glenageary, Co. Dublin. Tel: 01-2304343.

Dalkey Design Company, 20 Railway Road, Dalkey, Co. Dublin. Tel: 01-2856827.
Danaher, Deirdre. Tel: 01-2880380.
Danish Design, 69 Main Street, Blackrock, Co. Dublin. Tel: 01-2789040.
Daunt, Daphne. Tel: 021-4357891.
David Skinner Wallpaper, www.skinnerwallpaper.com.
Davidson, Michael. Tel: 087-6645248.
Davies Bathrooms, 150 Harmonstown Road, Raheny, Dublin 5. Tel: 01-8511700.
Debenhams, Jervis Shopping Centre, Dublin 1
Ireland. Tel: (01-878 -222).
DéBros Marble Works, The Court, Ashbourne Industrial Park, Ashbourne, Co. Meath. Tel: 01-8353100.
Decibel. Tel: 01-2967164; www.decibel.ie.
Dekko, 52 Boucher Road, Belfast BT12 6HR Tel: 028-90508600; www.shopdekko.com.
Delgrey Kitchens, Kilcoole, County Wicklow. Tel: 01-2871072; www.delgrey.ie.
Dempsey, Paul. Tel: 087-6660064.
Des Kelly, branches countrywide; www.deskellycarpets.ie.
Design Classics Direct www.designclassicsdirect.com
Design Flow, Unit 1B, Distillery Court, 537 North Circular Road, Dublin 7. Tel: 01-8349712; www.designflow.ie.
Design House, 8 Railway Road, Dalkey, Co. Dublin. Tel: 01-2352222 and branches in Derry and Belfast; www.designhousedublin.com.
Diamond Living, Longmile Road and Airside Retail Park, Swords. Tel: 1850-454444.
Domino Design (Wicklow). Tel: 01-286 6094; www.dominodesign.ie).
Donaldson & Lyttle, 114 Lower George's Street, Dún Laoghaire. Tel: 01-2808454 and 11a Boucher Retail Park, Belfast. Tel: 028-90667333.
Donegan Lighting Design Partnership. Tel: 01-6705022.
Dowling, Andy, Tel: 021-4963469.
Drawing Room, Westbury Mall, Dublin 2. Tel: 01-6772083.
Dream Beds, 65 Francis Street, Dublin 8. Tel: 01-4546626.

Drumm, Dennis. Malahide, Co. Dublin. Tel: 01-8452819.
Drumms, 15 Western Industrial Estate, Dublin 12. Tel: 01-4604335; www.drumms.ie.
Dublin Architectural Salvage Company. Tel: 01-4734368.
Dublin Furniture Company, 55 Capel Street, Dublin 1. Tel: 01-8728374.
Duff Tisdall, Mill Street, Dublin 8. Tel: 01-4541355 and 537 North Circular Road, Dublin 1. Tel: 01-8558070; www.duff-tisdall.ie.
Duffy, Joshua. Tel: 01-4730390.
Dún Laoghaire Kitchen Centre, 8 Cumberland Street, Dún Laoghaire, Co. Dublin. Tel: 01-2300336; www.dunlaoghairekitchencentre.ie.
Dundrum Kitchens, Apollo Building, Dundrum Road, Dublin. Tel: 01-2898709.
Dunnes Home, South Great George's Street, Dublin 2, Cornelscourt, Dublin 18, and large Dunnes Stores branches countrywide.
Dunsany Home Collection, Dunsany Castle, Co. Meath. Tel: 046-9026202; www.dunsany.ie.
Dwell, M7 Business Park, Naas. Tel: 045-898134.

Ebony & Co, 39 Fitzwilliam Street Upper, Dublin 2. Tel: 01-6690970; www.ebonyandco.com.
Elegant John, 70 North Wall Quay, Dublin 1. Tel: 01-8658010; www.elegantjohn.ie.
Eminence, 52 Sandycove Road, Co. Dublin. Tel: 01-2300193; www.eminence.ie.
Enclosure, Southern Cross Business Park, Boghall Road, Bray, Co. Wicklow. Tel: 01-2765000.
Enniskerry Trading Company, The Square, Enniskerry, Co. Wicklow. Tel: 01-2866275.
Equinox, 32 Howard Street, Belfast BT1 6PF. Tel: 028 90230089.
Erco Lighting, 289 Harold's Cross Road, Dublin 6w. Tel: 01-4966177.
Eric Pearce. Tel: 023-49852; epearce@eircom.net.
Esther Sexton Antiques, 51 Francis Street, Dublin 8. Tel: 01-4730909.
European Living, 74b Kylemore Road, Dublin 10. Tel: 01-6269005.
Eve Home Accessories, Meridian Point, Greystones, Co. Wicklow. Tel: 01-2016358.

Fabrique Interiors, The Cottage, Main Street, Dunshaughlin, Co. Meath. Tel: 01-8421716 www.fabrique.ie.
Famous Furniture, Longmile Road, Dublin 12. Tel: 01-4050520.
Fassbinder & English, Old Fire Station, George's Place, Dún Laoghaire. Co. Dublin. Tel: 01-2360683; www.fassbinderenglish.com.
Fine, Kate. Tel: 01-6703699; www.finedesign.ie.
Fired Earth, 31 Lower Ormond Quay, Dublin 1. Tel: 01-8735362 and 20 Lower George's Street, Dún Laoghaire, Co. Dublin. Tel: 01-6636160.
Fisher & Paykel. Tel: 1800 625174; www.fisherpaykel.com.

Flair International. www.flairshowers.com

Flanagans Of Buncrana, Deerpark Road, Mount Merrion.Tel: 01-2880218.

Form & Line, Ranelagh, Dublin 6. Tel: 01-4911201.

Formality. The Cowshed, Glasthule Village, Co. Dublin. Tel: 01-2808071.

Framemakers, Stillorgan Industrial Estate, Blackrock, Co. Dublin. Tel: 01-2954500.

Freedman, Gillian. Tel: 01-6767782.

French Country Interiors, Co. Tipperary. www.theantiquewarehouse.ie

French Warehouse, www.french-warehouse.com. Tel: 028-44839360.

Furnishing Distributors, 7 Bray South Business Park, Killarney Rd, Bray, Co. Wicklow. Tel: 01-2765811.

Furniture Designs, Old Bawn Road, Tallaght, Dublin 24. Tel: 01-4515326.

Gallagher, Alan. Tel: 087-2265362.

Gallagher, Alanna. alannagallagher@eircom.net.

Galleria, 61 South William Street, Dublin 2. Tel: 01-6744736; branches in Cork and Galway.

Gallery 29, 29 Molesworth Street, Dublin 2. Tel: 01-6425784.

Garuda Design, Maxol Building, 261-3 Ormeau Road, Belfast BT17 3GG. Tel: 028-90692626; www.garudadesign.com.

George Stackpoole Antiques, Adare, Co. Limerick. Tel: 061-396409.

Gerflor (Carrickmacross, Co. Monaghan. Tel: 042-9661431; e-mail: gerflorirl@gerflor.com) .

Glass Centre, The, Goldenbridge Industrial Estate, Inchicore, Dublin 8. Tel: 01-4541711.

Glen O'Callaghan Carpets, 131b Slaney Road, Dublin Industrial Estate, Glasnevin, Dublin 11. Tel: 01-8601849.

Global Village, Blackrock Shopping Centre, Co. Dublin. Tel: 01-2835550 and Powerscourt House, Enniskerry, Co. Wicklow. Tel: 01-2046087; www.globalvillage.ie.

Grange Carpet & Bedding, Deansgrange, Co. Dublin. Tel: 01-2896600.

Granny's Bottom Drawer, 53 Main Street Kinsale, Co. Cork. Tel: 021-4773616.

Greg Kinsella Interiors, Parnell Road, Bray, Co. Wicklow. Tel: 01-2868017; www.gregkinsella.ie.

Habitat, 6-10 Suffolk Street, Dublin 2. Tel: 01-6771433; Fairgreen Road, Galway. Tel: 091-569980; and 41 Arthur Street, Belfast BT1 4GB. Tel: 028-90249522.

Hafele, Kilcoole Industrial Estate, Co. Wicklow. Tel: 01-2873488.

Harkin, Tony. Tel: 087-2227372.

Harriet's House, 60 Dawson Street, Dublin 2. Tel: 01- 6777077 and 30 Blackrock Shopping Centre, Co. Dublin. Tel: 01-2884822.

Haus, Crow Street and Pudding Row, Temple Bar, Dublin. Tel:, 01-6795155; www.haus.ie.

Hearth & Home, Fonthill Retail Park, Dublin 22. Tel: 01-6200100; www.hearthandhome.ie.

Helen Turkington, 47 Dunville Avenue, Ranelagh, Dublin 6. Tel: 01-4125138.

Henderson, Roland. Tel: 086-2642743.

Herman Wilkinson, Rathmines, Dublin 6, 01-4972245.

Hicken Lighting, 17 Lower Bridge Street, Dublin 8. Tel: 01-6777882.

Hickeys Home Focus. Tel: 01-8208390.

Hickeys Fabrics, branches countrywide. Tel: 01-2845079 for details.

Hilary Roche Home, Unit A, Glencormack Business Park, Kilmacanogue, Co. Wicklow. Tel: 01-2723730; www.hilaryrochehome.ie.

Hogan Kitchens, Beechmount Industrial Estate, Navan, Co. Meath. Tel: 046-9022374; www.hogankitchens.com.

HOK, Blackrock, Co. Dublin. Tel: 01-2885011.

Hollands, Street Patrick's Woollen Mills, Douglas, Cork. Tel 021-4898000.

Home Store, Jervis Street, Dublin 1. Tel: 01-8726728.

Homes in Heaven, 2 Anglesea Buildings, George's Street, Dún Laoghaire, Co. Dublin. Tel: 01-2802077.

House of Fraser, Dundrum Town Centre Dublin 14. Tel: 01-2991400.

House of Ireland, 37 Nassau Street, Dublin 2. Tel: 01-6711111.

Houseworks, 11-15 Upper Erne Street, Dublin 2. Tel: 01-6769511; www.houseworks.ie.

Ideal Bathrooms, Lower Ballymount Road, Walkinstown, Dublin 12. Tel: 01-4609911; www.idealbathrooms.com.

Ikea, www.ikea.co.uk.

Imagine Wallpaper, Mall House, Thomastown, Co. Kilkenny. Tel: 056-7724760; www.imaginewallpaper.com.

Inreda, 71 Lower Camden Street, Dublin 8. Tel: 01-4760362; www.inreda.ie.

Inside Interiors, 3 Heather Rd, Sandyford Industrial Estate, Dublin 18. Tel: 01-2943869.

Inside Out, 97 Lower George's Street, Dún Laoghaire, Co. Dublin. Tel: 01-2148685.

Institute of Professional Auctioneers and Valuers. Tel: 01-6785685.

Instore, Limerick. Tel: 061-416088; Waterford. Tel: 051-844882; Galway. Tel: 091-530085 and Sligo. Tel: 071-9149174.

Interior Library, 6 Shelton Drive, Kimmage Road West, Dublin 12. Tel: 01-4059856.

Interior Touch, 67 Convent Road, Dún Laoghaire, Co. Dublin. Tel: 01-2809044 www.interiortouch.ie.

Interiors Bis, The Barn, Yeomanstown, Carragh, Naas, Co. Kildare. Tel: 045-856385; e-mail: interiorbis@eircom.net.

James, Helen. hjtextiles@eircom.net.

James Adam & Sons, 26 Street Stephen's Green, Dublin 2. Tel: 01-6760261.;

Jane Carroll, 62a Carysfort Avenue, Blackrock, Co. Dublin. Tel: 01-2783925.

Jenkins Interior Design, The Square, Cavan. Tel: 049-4331151.

Jennifer Goh, Landmark Court, Carrick-on-Shannon, Co. Leitrim. Tel: 071-9622208, www.jennifergohdesign.com.

Jenny Vander, 50 Drury Street, Dublin 2. Tel: 01-6770406.

Joe Vaughan Kitchens, Bellinter, Navan, Co. Meath. Tel: 086-8970219.

John Farrington, 32 Drury Street. Dublin 2. Tel: 01-6791899.

Johnston Antiques, 69–70 Francis Street, Dublin 8. Tel: 01-4732384, www.johnstonantiques.net.

Jones Antiques, 65-66 Francis Street, Dublin 8. Tel: 01-4546626.

Jungle Flowers, Malahide and Rush. Tel: 01-8454633.

JV Kitchens. Tel: 086-8336044.

KA International, Main Street, Blackrock, Co. Dublin. Tel: 01-2782033 and Jervis Shopping Centre, Dublin 1. Tel: 01-8781052; branches also in Cork, Galway and Enniskerry; www.kainternational.ie.

Kampf, Tony. Tel: 01-8214517.

KCR Joinery, Lower Kimmage Road, Dublin 6w. Tel: 01-4067672.

Keatings Fitted Furniture, Ballyhooley Road, Ballyvolane, Cork. Tel: 021-4506500; www.keatingfurniture.com.

Kelco Designs, Unit 18, Churchtown Business Park, Beaumount Avenue, Churchtown, Dublin 14. Tel: 01-2965500; www.kelcodesigns.com.

Kelly, Eva. Tel: 045-485389.

Kevin Kavanagh Gallery, 66 Great Strand Street, Dublin 1. Tel: 01-8740064.

Kevin Kelly Interiors, Morehampton Road, Donnybrook, Dublin 4. Tel: 01-6688533.

Kiernan, Eva, 18 Kildare Street, Dublin 2. Tel: 01-6629553.

Kilcroney Furniture, Bray, Co. Wicklow 01-2829361 www.kilcroneyfurniture.com.

Kilkenny Interiors, 8 Dean Street, Kilkenny. Tel: 056-7762450.

Kilkenny Living, Ballyhale, Co. Kilkenny. Tel: 056-7766796.

Kilkenny Shop, Nassau Street, Dublin 2; Market Cross, Kilkenny and High Street, Galway.

Kilkenny Tile Store, 7 Irishtown, Kilkenny. Tel: 056-7763099.

Kitchen Complements, Chatham Street, Dublin 2. Tel: 01 6770734.

Kitchen Flair, 6 Seafort Avenue, Sandymount, Dublin 4. Tel: 01-2695370.

Kitty Galore, 577 Lisburn Rd, Belfast BT9 7GS. Tel: 028-90681118.

Lamps & Lighting, I Terenure Road, Rathgar, Dublin 6. Tel: 01-49101-85

Laura Ashley, Grafton Street, Dublin, Blanchardstown and Cork.

Lavery Personalised Stationery, 01-4649829; www.lavery.ie.

Lawton, Terry. Tel: 028-4488870.

Lee, Angela. Tel: 01-4902307.

Lewendon, Sirin. sirin@sirinlewendon.com.

Light Plan, Penrose House, Penrose Quay, Cork. Tel: 021-4500665 and Richmond Road, Dublin 3. Tel: 01-8360200.

Lighting World, James's Street, Dublin 8. Tel: 01-6717788.

Lightworks, North Link Industrial Estate, Dundalk, Co. Louth. Tel: 042-9356014.

Limari, 7 Donnybrook Mall, Dublin 4. Tel: 01-2602420; www.limari.ie.

Limited Edition, 96 Francis Street, Dublin 8. Tel: 01-4531123.

Linen Berry, The, Geraldine Court, Maynooth, Co. Kildare. Tel: 01-6293094.

Linenmill, The Demesne, Westport, Co. Mayo. Tel: 098-29500; www.linenmillshop.com.

Little People, Ballyogan Road, Dublin 18. Tel: 01-2999796

Living Quarters, Bank House, Cornmarket, Dublin 8. Tel: 01-6717998.

Living, South William Street, Dublin 2. Tel: 01-6751898; and Castle Street, Bray, Co. Wicklow. Tel: 01-2828905.

L'Occitane, Wicklow Street, Dublin 2. Tel: 01-6797223, www.loccitane.com.

Lomac Tiles, 72 North Wall Quay Dublin 1. Tel: 01 8551588.

Lomi, Unit 124, Baldoyle Industrial Estate, Dublin 13. Tel: 01-8397001; www.lomi.ie.

Lynes & Lynes Antiques, 48a McCurtain Street. Tel: 021-4500982.

Mac's Salvage Warehouse, 749 South Circular Road, Islandbridge, Dublin 8. Tel: 01-6792110.

McAlinden, Helen. See No 6.

McCarthy, Pat, www.patmccarthystudio.ie.

McHenry Antiques, 1-7 Glen Road, Jordanstown, Newtownabbey, County Antrim. Tel: 028-90862036.

McKiernan, Peter. Tel: 01-2011901; 087-2436150.

McNally Kitchens/McNally Living, 46 Serpentine Avenue, Ballsbridge, Dublin 4 and M1 Business Park, Courtlough, Balbriggan, Co. Dublin. Tel: 01-6906000; www.mcnallyliving.com.

MacVeigh, Maria, mariamacveigh@ireland.com.

MacVeigh, Enriqueta. Tel: 085-7186022.

Maison, 46 Watergate Street, Navan, Co. Meath. Tel: 046-9066226.

Maplewood Design, 45 Avenue Road, Dublin 8. Tel: 01-4730579.

Marble & Granite Supplies, Coolock Industrial Estate Dublin 17. Tel: 01-8671077/

Marble & Lemon, Emmet Place, Cork. Tel: 021-4271877.

Martin Design. Tel: 086-2528166.

Martsworth Carpets, Ashford, Co. Wicklow. Tel: 0404-40113.

Material World, Church Terrace, Bray, Co. Wicklow. Tel: 01-2866668.

Mays, Laura. See Yaffe Mays Furniture.

Meadows & Byrne, The Pavilion, Royal Marine Road, Dún Laoghaire, Co. Dublin. Tel: 01-280 4554.

Mealys, Castlecomer, Co. Kilkenny. Tel: 056-4441229.

Merrion Square Interiors , 82 Merrion Square, Dublin 2. Tel:, 01-6761173; www.merrionsquareinteriors.com.

Michael Connell Antiques, 54 Francis Street, Dublin 8. Tel: 01-473 3898.

Milo Fitzgerald Interiors, Lavistown, Co. Kilkenny. Tel: 056-7771306.

mimo design, Fountainstown, Co. Cork. Tel: 021-4833443; www.mimodesign.ie.

Mimosa Interiors, Dún Laoghaire Shopping Centre. Tel: 01-2808166 and Cranford Centre, Stillorgan Road, Dublin 4. Tel: 01-2602443.

Minima, 8 Herbert Place in Dublin 2. Tel: 01-6627894; www.minima.ie.
Minnie Peters, 55 Upper George's Street, Dún Laoghaire, Co. Dublin. Tel: 01-2805965.
Mitofsky Antiques, 8 Rathfarnham Road, Terenure, Dublin 6. Tel: 01-4920033.
Mobilia, Drury Hall, Lower Stephen's Street, Dublin 2. Tel: 01-4780177.
Molloy Wood Crafts, Scariff Road, Whitegate, Co. Clare. Tel: 061-926000; www.molloywoodcrafts.ie.
Monogram Shop, The. Tel: 01-236 0311; www.monogram.ie .
Moore, Christopher. Tel: 087-2500380.
Mosaic Assemblers, Unit 14, The Courtyard, Fonthill Industrial Estate, Dublin 22. Tel: 01-6267669
Mosse, Nicholas. Bennetsbridge, Co. Kilkenny. Tel: 056-7727505.
MRCB Paints, 12–13 Cornmarket, Dublin 8. Tel: 01-6798755; Maynooth Road, Celbridge, Co. Kildare. Tel: 01-6303666; and Tramore Road, Waterford. Tel: 051-351299.
Mrs Greene for Cheeverstown, Templeogue, Dublin 6w. Tel: 01-4924867.
Muji, 5 Chatham Street, Dublin 2. Tel: 01-6794591.
Murphy, Joe. Tel: 086-8170151.
Murphy & Quinlan, Douglas Street, Cork. Tel: 021-4321021.
Murphy Sheehy, 14 Castle Market, Dublin 2. Tel: 01 6770316.
Myra Glass, New Street, Dublin 8. Tel: 01-4533321.

Narrow Space Gallery, The, Clonmel, Co. Tipperary; www.thenarrowspace.com.
National Lighting Centre, The, Upper Erne Street, Dublin 2. Tel: 01-676 9555.
Natural Interior, The, Mill Street, Dublin 8. Tel: 01-4737444.
Natural Wood Designs, Rathmiles, Killenard, Portarlington, Co. Laois. Tel: 057-8626483; 087-2761684.
Nelo Maternity, 39 Clarendon Street, Dublin 2. Tel: 01-6791336.
Nest, Unit 4, Midleton Enterprise Centre, Knockgriffin, Midleton, Co. Cork. Tel: 021-4630659; www.nest-design.ie.
Next, 67 Grafton Street Dublin 2. Tel: 01-6793300 and branches countrywide.
Niall Mullen Antiques, 105 Francis Street, Dublin 8. Tel: 01 4538948.
No 6, 6 Castle Market, Dublin 2. Tel: 01-6723904.
Noel Barry Joinery. Tel: 021-4652484.
NoLita, Unit 2 Cathedral Close, Tullow Street, Carlow. Tel: 059-9140231.
Nordic Living, 57 Main Street, Blackrock, Co. Dublin. Tel: 01-2886680.

O'Driscoll Furniture, 26-28 Lombard Street East, Dublin 2. Tel: 01-6711069; www.oddesign.ie.
O'Dwyer, Niall. Tel: 086-8237435.
O'Hagan Design, 102 Capel Street, Dublin 1. Tel: 01-8724016.
O'Neill, Sean. Tel: 087-2925114.
O'Sullivan Antiques, 43-44 Francis Street, Dublin 8. Tel: 01-4541143; www.osullivanantiques.com.
Oakline, 8 Ranelagh, Dublin 6. Tel: 01-

4977435: Unit 1, Greenhills Business Park, Tallaght, Dublin 24. Tel: 01-4626676; www.oakline.ie.
OBRE Fabrications, Milltown Industrial Estate, Rathnew, Co. Wicklow. Tel: 0404-69054.
Oman Antiques, 20-21 South William Street, Dublin 2. Tel: 01 6168991.
Oriental Rugs, 104 Francis Street, Dublin 8. Tel: 01-4531222.
Orior, 12 Greenbank Industrial Estate, Newry, Co. Down. Tel: 028-30262620; www.oriorbydesign.com.
O'Shea, Rick. Tel: 086-2616430.
Charles O'Toole, www.charlesfurniture.ie.
Oven Clean. Tel: 01-6615177; www.ovenclean.ie.
Oxfam Home, 86 Francis Street, Dublin 8. Tel: 01-4020555 and Bray, Co. Wicklow. Tel: 01-2864173.

Panelling Centre, The, 109 Longmile Rd, Walkinstown, Dublin 12. Tel: 01-4564899 and Sallynoggin Road. Tel: 01-2849988.
Peach Tree Upholstery, Hanover Road, Carlow. Tel: 059-9141624.
Pen Corner, The, 12 College Green, Dublin 2. Tel: 01-6793641.
Peoba, River Court, River Lane, Dundalk, Co. Louth. Tel: 042-9354222.
Period Design (Cavan). Tel: 049-9522323.
Peter Johnson Interiors, Cow's Lane, Temple Bar, Dublin 2. Tel: 01-6334325.
Peter Johnson (design), 6 Lombard Street, Dublin 8. Tel: 01-453088.
Peter Linden, George's Avenue, Blackrock. Tel: 01-2885875; www.peterlinden.com.
Pia Bang Home, 2 South Anne Street, Dublin 2. Tel: 01-8883777.
Plush Interiors, Balllast Quay, Sligo. Tel: 071-9154912.
Porter Ryle, Trafalgar Square, Greystones, Co. Wicklow. Tel: 01-2016379.
Project Office, 2 Exchange Street Upper, Dublin 8. Tel: 01-6715700.
Purple Ark. Tel: 087-6424166.

Quest Interiors, 37 Francis Street Dublin 8. Tel: 01-4540299.

Ray Shannon Headboards, 52 Cork Street, Dublin 8. Tel: 01-4532889.
Regan Tile Design, 2 Corrig Avenue, Dún Laoghaire, Co. Dublin. Tel: 01-2800921.
Renaissance, 114-116 Capel Street, Dublin 1. Tel: 01-8873809.
Renaissance Interiors, Stone Manor House, Naas Road, Rathcoole, Co. Dublin. Tel: 01-4587373.
Renu Bath, 78 Walkinstown Road, Dublin 12. Tel: 01-4500433.
Retrospect, Cow's Lane, Temple Bar, Dublin 2. Tel: 01-6726188.
Rice, Muriel and Noel. Tel: 01-4935303.
Robert Lee Ceramics, Durrus Road, Ballydehob, Co. Cork. Tel: 087-1271903; www.robertleeceramics.com.
Robert Scott Designs, 59 Capel Street, Dublin 1. Tel: 01 8740654; www.robertscottdesigns.com.
Rocca Stone and Marble, Unit 2, Site 21, Canal Walk, Park West, Dublin 12. Tel: 01-6205607; www.roccastone.com.
Rua, 1 Lower George's Street, Dún

Laoghaire, Co. Dublin. Tel: 01-2304209.
Rug Art, 49 Sandycove Road, Sandycove, Co. Dublin. Tel: 01-2360126; www.rugart.ie.
Rug Gallery, The, Coe's Road, Dundalk, Co. Louth. Tel: 042-9329851.

Scarff, Leo, www.jist.ie; www.leoscarffdesign.com.
Scotts, 124 Lower Baggot Street, Dublin 2. Tel: 01-6625680.
Scudding Clouds, www.scuddingclouds.com.
Seabourn Chic, The Murrough, Wicklow Town. Tel: 0404-64005; www.seabournchic.com.
Serendipity, 70 Rathgar Avenue, Dublin 6. Tel: 01-4968489.
Shaker Store, The, Ballitore, Co. Kildare. Tel: 059-8623372; www.shakerstore.ie.
Shannonside Kitchens, Street Nessan's Road, Dooradoyle Limerick. Tel: 061-228937.
Sharon Creagh Interiors, 57 Highfield Road, Rathgar, Dublin 6. Tel: 01-4970731.
Sheppards, Durrow, Co. Laois. Tel: 057-8636123.
Sherry Furniture, www.rossmorebysherry.com.
Sienna Design, 29 Patrick Street, Kilkenny. Tel: 056-7790771.
Signature Wood Flooring. Tel: 01-4299455; www.signaturewoodfloors.ie.
Simpson, Bill, e-mail: billsimpson@eircom.net.
Six Times Tables, www.sixtimestables.com.
SKI Interiors, Stephenstown, Brannockstown, Naas, Co. Kildare. Tel: 045-442866, www.skiinteriors.com.
Slattery, Liam. Tel: 01-4978446.
Snaidero, 41 Drury Street Dublin 2. Tel: 01-6794000.
Sofa Factory, The, Mill Street, Dublin 8. Tel: 01-4546877
Square Deal Interiors, Washington Street, Cork. Tel: 021-4274045.
Stafford, Karen, e-mail: karen@renovate.ie.
Stephenson, Karri. Tel: 01-6680398.
Still, Royston House, Upper Queen Street, Belfast BT1 6FA. Tel: 028-90466088.
Stock, 33 South King Street Dublin 2. Tel: 01-6794317.
Stone Developments, Ballybrew, Enniskerry, Co. Wicklow. Tel: 01-2862981.
Storage Solutions, 222 Harold's Cross, Dublin 6w. Tel: 01-4910714, www.storagesolutions.ie.
Summers, Nick. Tel: 01-8256132.
Sutton Fitzgibbon, Peter. Mountjoy Studios, 27 Mountjoy Square, Dublin 1. Tel: 087-2503140; www.decorativepainting.net.
Sweeney O'Rourke, 34 Pearse Street, Dublin 2. Tel: 01-6777212

TC Matthews Carpets, Greenhills Road, Walkinstown, Dublin 12. Tel: 01-4503822.
Thornby Hall, Millbrook, Naas, Co. Kildare. Tel: 045-901551; www.thornbyhall.ie.
Timlin, Gregor. www.gregortimlin.com.
Tipperary Furniture Company, Clonoulty, Cashel, Co. Tipperary. Tel: 0504-42493; www.tipperaryfurniture.com.

Touchwood, 35 Hamilton Street, South Circular Road, Dublin 8. Tel: 01-4539711.
Town & Country, 46 McCurtain Street, Cork. Tel: 021-4501468.
Town & Country, Lower Ormond Quay, Dublin 2. Tel: 01-8727401.
Traditional Designs, Bushfield Ave, off Marlborough Rd, Donnybrook, Dublin 4. Tel: 01-4126055.
Triple Star, www.triplestar.com.
Tru Curve, Grand Canal Business Centre, Dublin 8. Tel: 01-4730710.

Urban Outfitters 4 Cecilia Street, Dublin 2. Tel: 01-6706202.

V'soske Joyce, Oughterard, Co. Galway. Tel: 091-552113.
Versatile Bathrooms, Beechmount Industrial Estate, Navan, Co. Meath. Tel: 046-9029444; www.versatile.ie.
Victorian Salvage & Joinery Company, South Gloucester Street, Dublin 2. Tel: 01-6727000.
Villa & Hut, 79 Main Street, Gorey, Co. Wexford. Tel: 053-948116; www.villaandhut.com.
Villa Mia, Trim, Co. Meath. Tel: 046-9486717.
Vobe Interiors, Carrick-on-Shannon and Mullingar; www.vobeinteriors.ie.

Warehouse 39. www.w39.ie
Wetherley's, Unit 1, Deansgrange Business Park, Co. Dublin. Tel: (01) 2899110.
Wheelchair Association, The, Broadmeadows, Newcastle Road, Lucan, Co. Dublin. Tel: 01-6302479.
Whitewood and Linen, Unit 32, Naas Town Centre, Co. Kildare. Tel: 045-856482.
Wide Plank Floors, Unit 2-5 Albany Business Park, Kilcoole Industrial Estate, Co. Wicklow. Tel: 01-2760021.
Wild Child, 61 South Great George's Street, Dublin 2. Tel:, 01-4755099.
William Free, Meadowbrook Mews, Ballinteer Road, Dublin 16. Tel: 01-6684763.
Williams, Jane. Tel: 087-7819965.
Willie Duggan Lighting, Rose Inn Street, Kilkenny. Tel: 056-7764308; www.williedugganlighting.com.
Wink Lighting. Tel: 01-2836700 www.wink.ie.
Woodies DIY, branches countrywide.
Woodworkers, 1–10 Mount Tallant Avenue, Dublin 6w. Tel: 01-4901968.

Yaffe Mays Furniture, Salruck, Renvyle, Co. Galway Tel: 095-43089; www.lauramays.com.
Yard, The, Montgomery Road, Belfast. Tel: 028-90405600; www.theyard.co.uk.
Yesterday Once More, 3 Carysfort Avenue, Blackrock, Co. Dublin. Tel: 01-2108410; www.yesterdayoncemore.ie.

Zebrano, 91 Francis Street, Dublin 8. Tel: 01-4548750.